Soul
Of A
Slave

Madison Washington
and
The Creole Mutiny

By
Charles J. Boyle

St. John's Press
Tuscaloosa, AL

This book was previously published as an Amazon eBook under the title: "Madison Washington and The Creole Mutiny." Only the title and a few editorial changes have been made to this new issue.

Soul of A Slave: First Edition, First Printing

ISBN 978-0-9916014-5-5

St. John's Press, P.O. Box 572, Cottondale, AL 35453

www.stjpress.com

DEDICATION

For all who have suffered the pain of slavery

And

For my grandchildren: Alisa, Don, Amy, Jillian, Mallory, Griffin, Davis, Baylee, and Gary. You bring me peace and warm my heart.

My deepest appreciation to the students of Clinton High School, Clinton, Louisiana, who inspired me to write this book. From 1993- 2004, I was privileged to know, to teach, and to admire them all. In that little cubby hole just north of Baton Rouge, I met some of the finest young people in America. I thought they could use another hero, another role model to help guide them through life; hence, *Soul of A Slave, Madison Washington and The Creole Mutiny*.

CONTENTS

ACKNOWLEDGMENTS

Information used in the development of this novel was principally derived from a Masters of Arts Thesis written by William Joseph Poole, Jr. at Louisiana State University in New Orleans, LA, 1970. His research and written essay stands as the most detailed account of the mutiny aboard the Creole. His thesis may be reviewed at the Earl K. Long Library, (LSUNO) New Orleans, LA.

Other works detailing the account of the mutiny aboard the brig Creole are found in the Louisiana Commercial Court (Orleans Parish). These legal briefs reveal the entire history of the Creole mutiny. They are available on microfilm from the Earl K. Long Library, (LSUNO) New Orleans, LA.

The insurance lawsuits relating to the slave mutiny aboard the brig Creole, 1841, are important sources of information detailing the entire episode of the Creole affair. They are contained in the following docket numbers:

#4408: Thomas McCargo v. The Merchants Insurance Company. of New Orleans
#4409: Thomas McCargo v. The New Orleans Insurance Company
#4410: Edward Lockett v. The Merchants Insurance Company of New Orleans
#4411: Edward Lockett v. The Fireman's Insurance Company of New Orleans
#4413: Andrews and Hatcher v. Ocean Insurance Company
#4414: Sherman Johnson v. The Ocean Insurance Company
#4419: John Hagan v. The Ocean Insurance Co.

Some of the most extensive writings about the Creole affair can be found in Henry Wilson's *History of The Rise and Fall of the Slave Power in America* (3 vols., Boston, n.d. I, 443-452.

Frederick Douglas', *The Heroic Slave, Autographs for Freedom*, Boston, 1853, contains a short story describing Madison Washington and his quest for freedom.

There are many Newspaper accounts of the Creole mutiny: The example used in this story is from The *New Orleans La Courrier da la Louisiana*, December, 1841, (New Orleans public library).

PREFACE

I confess to having taken great liberties in writing this fictionalized account of Madison Washington and The Creole Mutiny. Very little is known about this epic figure in African American history. What evidence exists as to his stature, elocution, and bold character comes from the scant writings about him by the authors listed in the Acknowledgments, and the court documents that ensued sometime after the mutiny.

This author had the honor to serve as a teacher for more than twenty-five years in predominantly minority high schools in the south. Every February, Black History Month, students at these schools did their best to resurrect the deeds of, and honor the contributions of famous Black Americans. Their assemblies, reenactments, speeches, artwork and sometimes school plays, were well illustrated and served a useful purpose. Yet, as each year passed, these genuine displays of sentiment for Black heroes seemed to become somewhat outdated and a bit timeworn. Year after year, the students presented the same heroes as models of Black achievement. African American poets, inventors, scientists, Justices, and Soldiers—and many more significant characters of the past—were all given first class treatment by the students; but nothing new surfaced. As important to the development of Black pride and self-image that these historical figures are, the litany of heroes was becoming a little too repetitive and uninspiring. Surely, there must be more we can say, I mused.

By coincidence, while researching a different theme in the State Library of Louisiana in Baton Rouge, I inadvertently stumbled onto Louisiana newspaper items dated in the fall and winter of 1841. In bold print, they revealed the audacity of Madison Washington and the rebellion aboard the Creole. I was fascinated! I had never heard of him. I started asking questions.

A charming librarian there, steered me on to the Public Library of New Orleans where I was allowed to read a cardboard box full of court documents, research papers, and much more about Madison. I read until closing time, and returned many times thereafter, coming away with the seeds of this novel in my mind. It would add another gallant figure to the history of African American struggles and I couldn't wait to write his story.

Sadly, there is not much known about the day to day life of Madison Washington. That he was of great physical stature, was eloquent in his speech, did in fact foment a rebellion aboard the Creole and was released from custody by order of Queen Victoria, are indisputable facts. That he escaped from slavery, traveled to Canada and voluntarily returned to the south in order to rescue his wife, is also well documented. But reading court documents, one-hundred and fifty-year old newspaper accounts and ship logs, doesn't much interest high school students or anyone for that matter. I decided to novelize his story as you will read it here. I apologize if I have misled you or bogusly stirred your emotions. Someone had to write this story and bring Madison Washington to life.

Charles J. Boyle

Chapter One

Stonebreaker

The elderly and somewhat stooped black lady kneels before the several occupants of a cramped horse stall. An audience of six or seven spectators stand quietly behind her. Fresh straw masks the aroma of sweat and nearby manure. A mother's cry fills the air, followed by a few groans, a burst of exhaled air, and then silence. In a moment, a baby's first whimper is heard. Hands reach out, passing the swaddled newborn baby to the Grandmother.

Kianti Kitchens knew the Ashanti traditions of her native Africa better than anyone of the assembled group. She took the infant outside into the night, held him aloft to a crescent moon, and shouted ancient prayers of thanksgiving and promises of tithes in her native tongue. She returned to the stall and handed the baby back to the still perspiring, but smiling mother. "He is now sanctified and a child of God, Rebecca. He will be your protector. Do whatever you must to mold this son of Africa into a man. He will be the one to break this stone that hangs so brutally around our necks."

Thus, Madison Washington, first born of Rebecca and Isaac Washington, began life as a slave during the winter of 1819 in Virginia, near Halifax. But in reality, he was the property of Mr. Thomas McCargo, a plantation owner and merciless slave holder. A strong and robust infant, Madison adapted well to his surroundings and flourished, in spite of the harsh conditions of McCargo's pens. Rebecca, his teenage mother, trusted that her prayers were heard and was certain that she would have a boy soon after she became aware that she was pregnant. In defiance of the slave master's rules, she secretly named him "Bula Matadi," a Congolese term for the strong and hardy tradesmen known as "Breakers of Stone."

Rebecca Washington was the granddaughter of Kianti Kitchens, an African midwife and teacher, captured from her Ashanti village along the Ivory Coast in 1784 and sold into slavery. Kianti was an intelligent, proud, and attractive woman, passing those attributes and other talents along to her descendants.

Rebecca carried the Kitchens family name and their natural good looks. Her smooth light skin, full lips, and dark olive eyes immediately drew attention to her youthful figure. As a teenager, she was often forced to fend off the amorous advances of young men, both black and white. Her sharp tongue and iron will served to deter even the most aggressive suitors. Her instincts made her naturally suspicious of the McCargo sons and hired overseers. She blended into the background when they approached and sought refuge in the barns and outhouses of the plantation. "I am not ready for a man to rule me," she told her grandmother. "I see how they have treated you and how they treat all women; like we are their whores and are as dumb as stumps."

"I know what you are saying, Child." Grandma Kitchens said. "But you'll see; someone will come along that will capture your heart, just like your granddaddy stole mine. When that happens, you'll take back all the harsh words you been handing out to the boys."

The old woman paused and stared long at Rebecca. "I still miss Grandpa. I last saw him when they took us from our village. He didn't scream or cry… He just struggled and fought back hard, like an Ashanti warrior. Maybe I'll see him before I die."

"And my mother… my father?" Rebecca asked. Where are they now? I hardly remember them."

"I was carrying your mother when they took me. I gave birth on board the vessel that brought us here. She was a strong baby and we survived… I don't know how. Not long after you came along, both your Momma and Poppa were sold to a plantation in Mississippi… or maybe it was Alabama… I don't really know. You were too young to travel so they let me keep you.

"*Let* you keep me? Damn them, damn them all!"

"Careful what you say, Child. Hot words won't help you any. Pray for a savior to take us to freedom, like Moses done for his people."

Rebecca turned seventeen the summer of 1804. She had blossomed into a mature and beautiful woman, but was still not interested in any of the young men of the plantation. That is, until Isaac Washington came strolling down the path leading to the barn. She watched his approach with wonderment and awe.

Rebecca turned to several of her girlfriends, resting idly in the hay. "Come here, Sissy, she called to her best friend. Look-a-there… who is that?"

"I don't know," Sissy answered, "but he looks

like a mighty strong bull … walking straight up on two fine lookin' legs."

"He ain't from around here," another girl said. "But I hope he stays awhile. He be the handsomest man I ever did see."

Rebecca reacted: "Quick, everybody. Get to working at something. He's coming in here. Act like you don't notice and be giving him the big head."

Rebecca grabbed a pitchfork and began turning hay in one of the stalls. The other girls followed her lead. They were giggling uncontrollably when Isaac strode through the wide entrance. He stopped abruptly when he saw them, almost embarrassed to be in the midst of the girls. "What are you doing here?" Rebecca called to him, leaning on her tool. "You lost or something?

"I come to fetch harnesses for Massa's carriage horses," Isaac spoke shyly.

"They be hanging on them pegs," Sissy replied and pointed at the racks of leather goods. "You new here? I ain't see you 'afore. Where you come from, Mister? … got a name?"

Isaac, recovered, stood tall and answered boldly. "I come out of Mississippi… place called "The Forks," if it's any of your business, Sister. He hefted several harness yokes to his broad shoulders. Name is Isaac… Isaac Washington. I came in yesterday on a wagon. I got to git back to the house. Massa says I go to the fields today"

Rebecca drew closer to him and half smiled. Well, Mr. Washington, welcome to McCargo's plantation. It's not an easy life here, but you look like you can handle it. I might see you in the fields… maybe."

Isaac nodded, turned, and strode from the barn. "And maybe I will see you, too, Pretty Lady," he spoke softly. "Maybe I will."

He stopped abruptly and turned back toward the barn. "Hey, what's your name?"

"Rebecca!"

"What's wrong with you?" Sissy demanded of Rebecca. "You know you don't work in no fields. We is housemaids, barns and garden workers. That cotton patch will make a dried up old woman out of you... right quick, too."

"I don't know, Sissy. I think I been hit with something. My heart almost pattered its way out of my bosom just a-looking at him."

That afternoon, Rebecca asked her overseer if she could join her grandmother at the granary, near the corn fields. "She's getting along in years, Suh. I could help her shuck more cobs and fill up a lot more of those baskets."

Permission was granted and the following morning found Rebecca alongside her Grandmother on the path to the sheds that housed the granary. There the corn was shucked, dried, and ground into flour. Some of it was taken to storage for winter feed for the animals and much of it was squeezed for cooking oils. In fact, corn was the third largest crop on McCargo's holdings. Corn on this plantation was not intended so much for barter, but to sustain the livestock and provided food for both the slaves and the slave owner. As everywhere in Virginia and across the south, cotton remained king. But the buying and selling slaves seemed to dominate McCargo's interests these days, and it was the second largest producer of income for him.

For several years during harvest, Kianti Kitchens, along with a dozen older women, had worked their fingers to the bone, stripping the husks of corn, exposing and cleaning the "silk" from the ears, and sorting the cobs into mounds for drying and later milling. Younger and more able slaves carried it to the grist mill, where in a few weeks, it would be ground into flour. It was tiresome work, lasting from daylight to dark, and Grandma Kitchens was glad to have Rebecca along this day.

"You are such a thoughtful child, Rebecca. I'm glad you asked the driver. I been needin' to rest more during the day … get dizzy sometimes."

Rebecca grabbed her grandmother's hand. "Um hum." I'll be right beside you, Grandmamma."

It was late summer in the Virginia farmlands just east of the Tidewater. Steady rains, abundant sunshine, and cool weather had brought a plentiful corn crop this year. All the focus of the grist mill slave laborers was on stripping the corn, nothing else. It took about a week, but eventually Rebecca spotted him. He was driving a team of two dappled horses with an overloaded wagon of ripe cobs. Another driver sat beside him while Isaac handled the reins. "Whoa, big fellows," Isaac commanded. "Whoa, now."

Isaac skillfully brought the wagon to a halt adjacent to the granary doors. He and the other man began hefting large baskets of corn onto their shoulders and walked into the building. He saw Rebecca and smiled.

"Set your load over here," Grandma Kitchens directed. She pointed to a spot near where Rebecca was standing. "Set 'em down easy, like."

Isaac complied and with each load, he gazed momentarily at Rebecca, always smiling. Finally, when the task was completed, he asked. "Can a man get a drink of water around here?"

"I'll get you some," Rebecca shouted and made a run for the door and out to the well. She quickly tripped over her feet; feeling quite foolish as Isaac extended his hand, laughed, and helped her to her feet.

"I'm sorry," she mumbled and brushed off her clothing. "I guess I look pretty silly, huh?" Small tears gathered at her eyes.

"No, Missy… you look just fine to me. Now let's have that water."

They strode to the well together, quietly, and Rebecca, recovered from her embarrassment, drew a ladle of cool water. She handed it to him and he covered her hand on the handle. Rebecca felt a chill run through her. "Call me Rebecca, not 'Missy'"

"That I will, Rebecca. Is that your Grandma over there? …think she'd mind if I came around now and again?"

"What for?"

"I'd like to know you a little better. Why, I might could teach you to run without falling all over yourself." .

Rebecca slapped him playfully on the arm and he feigned injury. "Ow! Your Grandma be a lookin'. Now don't get me in no mess."

"If Grandma isn't out here already, a-whupin' your big self, I guess she approves of you. I suppose you can come 'round after chores. We live in the shed next to the barn."

I know where you live, Rebecca. I been knowing since I first laid eyes on you. I have to get back to the fields, now. Watch for me tonight."

Isaac put his arm around her waist and walked her the few steps back to granary doors. Rebecca felt the urge to do likewise, but knew that her grandmother was watching them both.

Isaac left on the wagon and Rebecca faced her grandmother. "Well, what do you think, Grandmomma?

He wants to come a-courting."

"I told you somebody would come along and steal your heart, Rebecca. Only you can say for sure, but that might be him. Keep your head clear, like I taught you and we'll see if he's a decent man."

Isaac arrived at Rebecca's lodgings shortly after dark, carrying an arm load of fresh fruits and vegetables. She had put on a pretty gingham "church" dress that some-one had handed down to her. She had fashioned her hair in a bun and had washed the day's dust from her body. She glowed with the light of teenage innocence, and Isaac, when he saw her, gasped. *I swear, I am in the presence of a goddess.*

Grandmother Kitchens, Rebecca, and Isaac sat around an oaken table, measuring each other in the glow and flicker of candlelight. They learned that Isaac thought he was about nineteen or twenty years old; he wasn't sure. He was orphaned early in life and never knew his parents. He professed a belief in a white Jesus and assured them that He would come again to rescue them from this "contempt-ible" life of slavery. He admitted that he had surrendered to the white masters, but only under the sting of the whip. "I been whupped more times than I can count... I finally buckled and now I bide my time; waitin' to be saved. I don't start any mess with the drivers and overseers. I do my chores and they leave me be. Lord have mercy!"

At some point, Grandma Kitchens slipped off to a tick mattress in a corner of the room. It had been her bed for twenty years. She began to snore, softly at first, and then louder and louder.

Isaac blew out the candles, took Rebecca's hand and they slipped out of the door and into the soft glow of a full moon. They didn't notice the one, wide open eye of

Grandmother Kitchens peering at them through the darkness. "Praise the Lord... that's him she muttered." She rolled over and went to sleep.

Rebecca and Isaac strolled hand in hand along the fences and garden plots of the slave quarters. They spoke only of the future and the promises that it might hold. Eventually, they found themselves outside the compound and wandered into a field of daisies, sunflowers, and marigold. They sat beneath the mammoth branches of a southern magnolia tree, rich with white blossoms, weeping from the accumulating nighttime dew. There, Isaac kissed her and Rebecca respond with a sense of youthful passion, arising out of her soul.

Madison Washington was conceived there in that meadow, in a glorious setting between earth and heaven. "He will be a boy" Rebecca offered. And he will take us to freedom.

"You are a dreamer," Isaac countered, "but a beautiful dreamer for sure. I love you, Rebecca Kitchens."

They married in the late summer of 1818, behind the sheds and corrals of McCargo's slave pens, out of sight of the Masters. Isaac and Rebecca jumped over a straw broom, in Ashanti fashion, sealing their commitment to one another. A small group of onlookers sang and clapped their approval. In the morning, Isaac returned to the fields and Rebecca accompanied her smiling grandmother back to the granary.

Chapter Two

Mississippi

In the summer of 1820, when he was six months old, Isaac, Rebecca, and Madison, along with a half dozen other slaves, were sold and transported by sailing vessel to a slave market in New Orleans. Desecrated and debased upon the auction block, they were sold as a family and began a foot journey northward along with two-dozen other slaves. They had no knowledge of where they were going or what their future might hold. Driven like cattle for nearly two hundred miles, they stumbled forward, zombie-like, covering some twenty-five miles a day.

Unaccustomed to the choking humidity of Louisiana, several slaves collapsed from exhaustion. Overseers on horseback said little and offered less in the way of water, food, or comfort. Not long after the trek began, they were forced to wade into a swamp, scrambling to board a flatboat about one hundred feet from the shore. One man was snake-bitten, but dragged along through the water by his chain and the strength of those to whom he was attached. He died that night, withering in pain, his limbs swollen to several times their size.

At Baton Rouge, Catholic missionaries came out and conferred with the overseers. A camp was established and the body laid to rest the following morning. A young priest officiated, calling upon his savior to "snuggle the dead man to His warm and merciful bosom."

After some heated conversation between the head Friar and the overseers, the slaves were unshackled and given drink, sweet meats, and biscuits. They rested for a day, then lumbered northward until nightfall, finally making camp near the start of a road made of felled timber. "Plank Road," someone called it.

"That preacher musta' had some powerful words for them devils," a middle-aged female slave offered. "I made a coffle or two 'afore. I ain't never had no mercy from any of them white heathens."

"It weren't the praying," another lady replied. "We are the property of Massa' Charles King. I hear he be known to fear the Lord and he don't wanna' rile Him."

The following morning, guards unshackled the slaves and provided scant, but adequate provisions. They were given Johnny cake or pone and a pasty white concoction the guards called "Camp Gravy." It was tasteless, but mixed with the bread and scraps of ham or other meats, the food served to nourish the slaves.

They trudged on for another three days, finally arriving at Kingland, the Charles King plantation near Woodville, Mississippi. Rebecca Washington had carried her baby on her back all the way, swaddled in a colorful bandanna.

The coffle of slaves emerged from a wooded pine forest and approached Kingland from the crest of a small hill. Rebecca and Isaac were immediately struck by its grandeur. Directly ahead of them stood a huge white-columned mansion of regal proportions. Rebecca gasped slightly when she saw it. Fifty live oak trees lined each side of the long wide path leading up to the house. Their full branches stretched out across the road, embracing, like lover's arms. A luxurious red rose garden blossomed at the foot of the porch, contrasting pompously with the menagerie of leafy green philodendrons, white baneberry, and yellow buckeye.

"Isaac... Look there. I've never seen—"

"We sure is a long way from Virginee. Why, lookin' at all of this, you might say that Massa' McCargo's plantation was just a white man's dirt farm."

Waiting for all of the slaves to assemble on the hillside, Rebecca eyes fixed on the panorama that lay before her: Kingland, the richest plantation in all of Mississippi.

The mansion's foundation was made of white masonry, fashioned from natural limestone that had been dragged by mule and sled from the surrounding country-side. It was three-storied, with a small garret topping it off. The house rose straight up from a sea of pea-green grass, freshly mowed by scythe and sickle. Facing it from the south, eight Roman columns festooned the broad front porch, supporting a second story balcony. Rebecca counted eighteen windows across the front and wondered what human delights occurred behind them.

Some one-hundred yards behind the mansion, fifty long white cabins stood in neat rows, enclosed by a three beam, split rail fence. Smoke from cooking fires rose slowly into the sky, drifting toward the slaves waiting on the hill and emitting scents of roasted pork, fresh baked bread, and steaming vegetables. A few men and women, all black and all slaves, moseyed here and there about the place, carrying bundles of firewood, garden produce, and other commodities from the gardens. Chickens pecked for morsels of food, while a lazy cur dog mothered her pups in a doorway.

A whip cracked and a command to "Get up and get on" obliterated Rebecca's assessment of Kingland. She groaned, slung Madison onto her back and obeyed. She walked hand in hand with Isaac toward an unknown future.

A scowling white man on horseback directed them into their new quarters and Rebecca and Isaac settled in. The small cabin they occupied was much roomier than the shed they knew at McCargo's. It was made of sturdy fat-pine boards, milled smooth and freshly whitewashed. Two open windows allowed a view to the east and west, granting an ample supply of sunlight for most of the day. At night and in foul weather they could be shuttered from within. A slate roof protected it from seasonal monsoon rains and Rebecca sensed no dampness within. Inside, an old pinewood bed pressed against the wall. Several wooden wash buckets, a rough looking table and a few chairs were scattered about the room.

"It has promise," Rebecca commented.

"How's the baby getting along?" Isaac asked as they settled into the cabin. "I'm fixin' to go find us some kindling… build a cook-fire."

He left the dwelling and retuned in about an hour with an arm load of firewood. "I met up with some of the others," Isaac reported. "Rebecca, we gonna' do all right here. They showed me around the place. Why, we got a store with provisions and dry goods. We can do some tradin' of goods with the other families. There's a possum trot over to the smokehouse and storeroom out back. We even got a three-hole privy, but we have to share with two other families."

Rebecca was less than interested in Isaac's description of the slave accommodations at Kingland; she had something else on her mind. She held her baby up, thrusting him forward into Isaac's face. "Look close at him, Isaac. He has a grand African name. He isn't 'The Baby' like you call him. He is Bula Matadi... Breaker of Stone!"

Isaac turned and dropped his load of firewood into a bin. He sighed, and then gazed at his beautiful young wife with her slim waist and full bosom. She was still breast-feeding Madison. "Aw, Rebecca... you know we ain't in Africa and we ain't African no more." Isaac retorted. "...been too long. We are in the white man's America, now. Why, lookin' at you, some folks think you might have a bit o' white in you," he teased.

Rebecca's skin was a light smooth color, akin to ginger. Her slender nose and wide glistening black eyes made her attractive to the slave merchants and had brought a higher price because of it. She was barely eighteen now, but she had long been aware that white men looked at her with something more than 'price per pound' in their eyes.

"My mother and father were African... Ashanti! His name is Bula Matadi. He is Ashanti, like me."

Isaac reached for his son and held him up. "I love ya'all, Rebecca. But Massa' King hear that name, he be having a hissy fit. They don't want no African names, just them bible names."

"Isaac, you hear me. Bula Matadi will set us free someday... break this stone around our necks and shatter it into a thousand pieces. Grandma Kitchen's said so."

Isaac frowned. "Don't stir up no trouble by talking 'bout freedom, Rebecca. Don't need it now. I been looking around. We have a good little cabin here... plenty of crops in the field. Folks say Massa' King a fair man ... might make a life here."

Rebecca took her baby from Isaac. Holding him beneath the armpits, she danced in circles, around and around the room. "Why, he already weighs a peck—"

"He is stout... be a good field hand."

"Look at him, Isaac. He has that broad forehead like you. He'll be smart... fearless like the African lion. He is never going to chop cotton... pick seed"

Isaac, twenty-one perhaps, had been a slave since childbirth. Strong and rebellious as a youth, he had surrendered his huge and hardened body to the white man after years of physical abuse. He faced Rebecca in exasperation. "He's going to be a slave just like you and me. Quit your dreaming about ever being free. Please, Rebecca. Madison don't need to have those notions in his head. It will only bring trouble for him."

Rebecca sat down in a straight-backed wooden rocking chair and nursed her baby. She'd soon have to put him on solid foods while she joined the other women in the sheds, picking the seeds from cotton or some other labor. Rocking him back and forth, she looked around the cabin, evaluating their new surroundings. A potbellied wood stove sat in the center of the room, a modern innovation. She had known only a brick fireplace at McCargo's.

There were several bins for food storage. A large wooden tub for washing clothes and for bathing stood on its edge against the wall. In spite of its primitive style, the sturdy pine bed looked comfortable with its cotton-stuffed mattress. She mentally gave thanks to the Lord. They had slept on straw in Virginia.

The many buildings of the King plantation slave quarters made up a small village of its own. A large garden flourished just inside a whitewashed split rail fence and ran the length of the cantonment. To Rebecca and Isaac, it was a vast improvement over the last farm they had lived on. The cupboards were stocked with rice, flour, and turnips. Slabs of salted pork filled a small barrel on top of the kitchen table.

In the afternoon of their first day, a welcoming committee of neighboring slaves delivered a basket of fresh eggs and vegetables. Someone handed Isaac several blankets and two boys wrestled a shaky wooden crib through the door. One by one, the women hugged Rebecca, and then praised her for delivering such a "fine looking baby boy." The men shook Isaac's hand, lit pipes and explained the routines of the plantation and the attitudes of the overseers.

"Mr. King, he don't come 'round much," one man said. "But you best be bending' over when that Rufus ride by."

When they had gone, Rebecca closed her eyes, nursing and rocking her baby. She was beginning to feel comfortable and she agreed with Isaac that perhaps they could enjoy some of God's blessings here. *But only if we can live free. Bula Matadi will do it…. My breaker of stones.*

Isaac busied himself bringing in more wood and straightening up the place, putting away clothes and blankets. They had arrived with two bulging carpetbags, holding all the personal belongings they were allowed to bring. Neighboring slaves provided the rest.

"This place sure beats all…. Folks are friendly… helping out. Yes, Suh… not bad at all," Isaac said.

Chapter Three

The Kings

Charles King, a balding, red-faced, roly-poly man of fifty-six, was a happy and contented landowner. He measured his wealth, not in the number of acres he cultivated, but in the number of slaves he owned. Even though he was a slaveholder, Charles feared the wrath of God, often vacillating between the needs of his plantation and the condition of his slaves.

"Make sure you provide sufficiently to their needs, Mr. Bohlinger," he often reminded Rufus, the head overseer. "No punishments without my consent."

Charles had inherited his wealth and land; therefore, he managed it with a scant eye toward the future. He accepted things as they were, disassociating himself with the day-to-day tasks of running the plantation. He seldom visited the fields, ginning houses, or barns. He gave full authority to Rufus, trusting that he'd follow his instructions to keep the slaves satisfied and in line.

Ruth King, Charles' bride, was now middle-aged and growing increasingly fat. She could bear no more children and that depressed her. She and Charles no longer slept together and she ached for the warmth of a touch—companionship other than her house servants. Her two older children had married and moved away. She was a natural and instinctive mother who looked to the bible for direction. Having children, producing souls for God, was her mission in life and she longed to have more.

"Those Niggra women breed like field mice and I am doomed to be forevermore unfruitful," She told Charles. "What wrong have I done?"

"But we have children, Ruth. I have heirs. We're beyond our time. I've neither the inclination nor the patience for rearing any more youngsters."

"It just isn't right. It's not fair, Charles. God's promise to Abraham was a blessing of many children, and if you look across that pasture you'll see who has been blessed."

Their conversation soon fell to discussing the possibility of bringing a slave child into the house. "Just to liven up the place," she begged Charles.

"A Negro child, Ruth! Is the ache inside you that awful? My God."

"Just look at Sarah.... It did not matter to God where Abraham's first child came from."

"If it means that much to you, I'll allow it. But the child must be sturdy and fair skinned. Perhaps we could groom one as a driver... household attendant."

"Oh, thank you, Charles."

"Ruth, you are obliged to make it known that you chose this slave child as your own house servant. My God... my church members would tar and feather me if they thought I had produced the thing."

"When might I bring this child into the house,

Charles? Soon, I trust."

"Well, there is an infant boy among the new pur-
chases that just arrived. We'll go down and take a look."

Rebecca and Isaac cleaned and prepared their
new lodgings. They would soon be in the fields from dawn
to dusk and there would be little time for housekeeping.
"Do those lanterns have oil?" Rebecca called to Isaac.

Footsteps beating a path to their door caused
her to halt in mid-sentence. She clutched Madison tightly.
Charles King, his wife, and several of their servants pushed
their way into the low dwelling. With his riding crop in
one hand, Charles removed his broad white hat with the
other. "Good morning, Mizz' Washington... Isaac. Ruth
here, ah... we came to see the baby. I'm told he's a top-
quality boy. Let me see the little rascal."

Rebecca removed Madison from her nipple and
turned him for the master and all to see. She covered herself
and stood, beaming as she held him up.

"He is full-sized, Mizz' Washington," Charles
King remarked. He leaned forward to inspect the child.
"He suffered no damage from your journey? The child is
fit... no sickness?"

"He's healthy, Massa'... always mighty hungry."

Good. We'll take him up to the house for a while;
give him a decent start. You too, Mizz' Washington. Get
your things... hurry, now."

Rebecca's heart raced and she stood frozen,
clutching her baby against her breast. Charles King motioned to the servants to take the baby.

"Does he have a name?"

"Madison... Madison Washington," Isaac said.

Rebecca glared at him. "He is Bula Matadi,"
she whispered.

Charles King waved his hat and slapped his crop against his leg. He was a loud and boisterous man, always animated when he had an audience. "Well, hot damn, Isaac. That's an excellent name. Ya'all know about our fourth president, do you? Why, he composed the Virginia Plan. It became our constitution, the heart of all our freedoms. That boy can be proud to have his name."

"Yes, Suh," Isaac said. "Gonna' name all my children' after presidents."

"Good. I'm mighty pleased. Now let's have that baby up to the house."

A young servant girl took the baby from Rebecca and wrapped him a blanket. Rebecca silently dug through the bags, gathering a few items of clothing. Ruth reached and took Madison from the girl. "Let me hold him while Mizz Washington makes ready. Yes, he is a delightful baby... good coloring." Ruth pinched his cheeks lightly and tickled him under the chin, cooing all the while.

"We'll go now," Charles King said. "You have work, Isaac... enough celebration for now. You may visit the house tonight when you come in from the field... around back." Charles King led the entourage from the cabin. He frequently spent a few minutes with new slave families, but he did not always invite their children into his home. Times had changed. In 1820 the price of a healthy slave was approaching six hundred dollars and going up.

"Why he just might be worth a thousand dollars or more by the time he can go into the fields," Charles mentioned to Ruth on the way back to the house. "I'll go to the clerk and file papers this afternoon... get insurance on him."

Madison Washington came along at a time in Ruth King's life when her craving for another child was at a peak. She doted over him, calling him, "My Lil' Maddy."

Charles accepted him with little comment. "It makes her less an aggravation to me," Charles explained to those who might inquire. He paid scant attention to Ruth, and less to Madison and Rebecca. He was more concerned with bird hunting, measuring his growing wealth, and his association with his church. "Ruth manages the household, but I preside over Kingland," he boasted among his friends. "Why, I might even run for Governor someday."

Chapter Four

The Kingland

The Kingland mansion was an opulent dwelling, structured similarly to early Grecian designs. The portico, adorned with huge sixth-century Ionic columns was made of imported Italian marble. Three stories up, a low, sloping roof topped the front of the house with six gables, front and back. A man took eight strides across the porch before touching the twelve-foot oaken double doors. The foyer accents announced the meticulous order of this house, every piece of imported furniture in perfect arrangement and sitting there as if no one had ever used it.

Within this strictly ordered household were eight rooms on the ground floor, among them a large kitchen, pantries, a luxurious dining room, several offices, a library, and a study. Each room presented furnishings from Europe; primarily French, but some Egyptian, with their perfume bottles and lamps. Bedrooms were set in a Victorian motif, as it was a popular custom of the day. Charles and Ruth both admired the young British Queen Victoria, and had once received a correspondence from her.

The framework of a mahogany spiral staircase, rising from the entrance hall, worked to endow every part of the house with interest and life. Charles often stood on the staircase, halfway up, turning to survey his possessions and feeling somewhat like an Egyptian Pharaoh himself.

The second floor hosted twelve rooms, running alongside a lengthy, tongue and grooved cedar hallway. Amid the many bedrooms were private baths, another library, a music room, and nursery. The third floor was likewise structured. It housed the servants, the drivers, nursemaids, cooks, and all other maintenance staff. It was here that Rebecca moved into a private room with her infant son.

She served as a cook and an excellent one at that. In her free time, she nurtured Madison as any mother would, but she knew he was the darling of Ruth King, and she silently cursed the woman. *Who does she think she is? Bula Matadi is my son.*

The King plantation was one of the largest in Mississippi. It covered some 3000 acres of cotton, corn, sorghum, timber and herds of fine cattle. Isaac, assigned to work in the grain fields, looked across the golden pastures through the eyes of a slave, but marveled at the splendor of it. Soft breezes bent the endless sea of corn fronds back and forth, altering the hue from green to light blue and back to green. Behind him, a blanket of white cotton stretched unbounded to the horizon.

The beauty of the scene hypnotized him. Finally, he reached down and gathered a handful of soil, sniffed it, and then broadcast it to the wind. "Deliver us, Jesus. Under your hands Bula Matadi gonna' break them stones, just like Rebecca says he will." He shouldered his scythe, walked briskly forward and merged with the other one hundred and twenty slaves who worked these fields from daylight to dark, making Charles King one of the richest men in Mississippi.

Madison hardly knew his father after that first day when Charles and Ruth took him to the main house. At first, Isaac visited each night after coming in from the fields, but cutting remarks from Ruth let him know that he was not as welcome as Charles King had implied. Once she shooed him out of the house with a broom, telling him that he smelled of manure and polluted the air around him. Later, she wrongly accused him of stealing a slice of pie from her pantry. For that, Rufus Bohlinger beat him with the handle of an ax.

Dispirited, Isaac seldom went to the house; meeting Rebecca and Madison from time to time in a barn or deep in the fields, out of sight of the white masters. Their meetings, although brief, were moments of joy for both Rebecca and Madison. Their love for one another never waned, in spite of the circumstances. Isaac doted over his son, bouncing him on his knee, holding him lovingly and whispering tales of ancient African grandeur in his ear. Conjugal relationships between Rebecca and Isaac were rare, sometimes out of the question due to the brevity and clandestine nature of their visits. Rebecca and Isaac had no more children.

Rufus Bohlinger, a harsh and arrogant man from Baker, Louisiana, was the principal foreman at Kingland. He wielded brutal totalitarian power over the slaves, as Isaac was doomed to learn. On a stormy spring day, a few years after their arrival, Rufus confronted Isaac in a barn as he shoveled manure from the stables. He accused Isaac of acting "uppity" as a result of his special relationship with Rebecca and the King household. " Have you been sneaking out to the fields with that woman o' yours? You have... ain't ya, Boy? You supposed to visit out back of the house, and only when I allow it. Now, you missed my head count yesterday evening, Boy."

Isaac, always subservient to his white masters, felt a twinge of anger, but held his fire in check. "But, Massa Rufus, my boy just wanted to be with his Poppa ... romp and play a bit. I didn't know you was a countin' heads. Didn't mean no disrespect, Suh."

"You disobey my rules, it calls for the whip, Boy. Turn around!" The headmaster raised his crop. "Turn your backside, I said."

Isaac had felt the sting of Rufus's lash before and the memory came back like a flash. Something snapped deep within him. "No, Suh... I ain't takin' no more a your whuppin's." He raised his arms to defend himself, blocking Rufus' first blow and the whip flew from Rufus's hand.

Enraged, he picked up a wooden stable post lying there and brought it across Isaac's side, knocking the wind from him and buckling his knees. Isaac fell, defenseless against the savage blows now being pummeled upon him. A final blow across the neck ended the beating for Isaac. He rolled onto his back, quivered for a few moments and then died, staring wide-eyed at his assassin. His whispered his final words: "Bula Matadi ... Bula Matadi."

Rufus Bohlinger leaned on his club, gasping for breath. Finally recovering, he threw the bloody weapon into a hay stack. He kicked Isaac's warm body, spit, and walked calmly out of the barn.

Isaac Washington, faithful husband, proud father, and man of perpetual optimism, died in the spring of 1828, broken in body and in spirit under the cruel yoke of slavery. Rebecca and Madison were told that he had suffered an accident.

"Fell out of the loft... broke his damn fool neck," Rufus explained.

No one could be certain, but suspicion surrounded the incident. To the slaves, it seemed that Rufus harbored a particular dislike for Isaac—obvious after Madison and Rebecca moved into the main house. Without witnesses or a sheriff's investigation, it didn't take much to make them believe that Rufus had killed Isaac, perhaps during one of his regular fits of rage. They whispered as much amongst themselves, the accusations finally reaching Rebecca and Madison.

Charles King became aware of the gossip and questioned Rufus briefly about the incident. "That boy was a stout worker, Rufus. I can't afford to lose slaves with a value as high as his. Insurance might not cover the loss. Tell me what happened."

Rufus took Charles to the barn and explained his version as to how Isaac had met his death. The bloody club was nowhere in sight, nor any other evidence of the beating. "His back was toward me, up there in the loft," Rufus pointed. "He musta' lost his hold and slipped. Big as he was, he hit the ground with a loud thump. I heard his neck crack. There weren't nothing I could do."

Charles accepted the explanation and the incident was not mentioned again. It never left the minds of the slaves, however, and they stayed clear of Rufus, never finding themselves alone with him and obeying his every command.

Rebecca and Madison stayed long beside Isaac's grave, silently mourning her husband and Madison's father well into the afternoon. *Bula Matadi will avenge you, my love. The wicked shall be punished in full measure to their evil deeds.*

She sifted a handful of black dirt over the mound, placed a rose at Isaac's head and walked hand in hand with Madison back to the King Mansion. *You were an honorable man, Isaac. I will love you forever. There will never be another.*

Chapter Five

The Teacher

When Madison was nearly nine years old, Rebecca asked Mrs. King if he could be allowed to learn to read. "Bible verses, at least."

"You wish to Christianize him… what faith.?" Ruth asked.

"Anglican… their missionaries baptized us in Virginia."

Mrs. King agreed and a teacher was summoned: an educated former slave, Miss Agnes Beauchamp-Jackson. She arrived in the summer of 1829, having driven her own buggy up from New Orleans. She presented her papers and assured Mrs. King that she was a free woman and a scholar of note.

Ruth was relieved that "Miss Agnes" was mulatto, with European features and clear speech. She was struck by Agnes' long lashes and piercing green eyes. Ruth fought the urge to admit that she was quite attractive and she felt somewhat inferior in her presence. The interview took place in the large foyer of the mansion. Miss Agnes seated herself on a colorful red and blue provincial settee. Ruth sat on a brightly colored causeuse, facing her. She gave instructions to a black attendant and had cold drinks prepared and brought to them. She had heard that Miss Agnes frequently rubbed elbows with high level politicians and the prominent citizens of New Orleans; therefore, she afforded her courtesies not usually granted to a Colored person.

"And your background?" Ruth inquired.

Miss Agnes did not smile, concealing her disdain for spoiled rich women such as Ruth King. She set her drink on a white starched doily and appraised her host. "I bit shot and loaded muskets for General Jackson during the siege at New Orleans. I was previously a cabin attendant aboard Jean Lafitte's Corvette. He favored me."

"My word," Ruth said blandly. She placed her glass on a table, her mouth open and her eyes fixed on this exotic woman. *What does she mean, "He favored me?" His damned whore, I suppose.*

"Please go on, Ruth stammered.

"All of us... freedmen, gamblers, Creoles.... We rallied and pushed the heathen Redcoats back into the sea. General Jackson emancipated me when we went up to Tennessee. I took his name."

"Do tell," Ruth replied and stood up. "Mr. Jackson may well be our next president. I don't have much time. I suppose you'll do as a teacher for Madison... strictly scripture, mind you."

Miss Agnes rose slowly, brushing off her bright velvet dress. "My wages?"

"Goodness, you require payment? I presumed rations and accommodations would suffice."

"I am not a slave, Mrs. King. Two dollars a

week... lodging and food... a little whiskey and tobacco from time to time. I do not perform chores."

"Well... I'll agree. My Lil' Maddy needs you. Take the room next to Rebecca." Ruth stood.

"I have not quite accepted the position, Mrs. King. What are your views... restrictions on Negro education, if any?"

"Strictly the Old and New Testaments. He may learn letters and to write simple sentences."

Agnes pursed her lips. "I must have greater liberty than that, Mrs. King. In your letter, you explained that Madison was like your own child. What mother would feed her son a snake when he asked for a fish?"

"I'm certain you will find ample evidence of such matters in the Bible, Madame. You appear to have read it. Feel free to innovate."

"Mathematics...? History? Literature?"

Ruth was frustrated. She was not accustomed to being quizzed by Coloreds, free or not. "What do you know of such things?"

"I am a practicing Methodist, schooled by the Reverend William Serrington when he was a guest of Mr. Jackson. I know much more than the Bible."

"Well then, draw upon your own background. Do what you must. This interview is over, Madam Beauchamp-Jackson. Now do you accept the position?"

Miss Agnes smiled for the first time. "It'll be my pleasure to serve as tutor for Madison. Where is my room and when can I meet the child?"

Miss Agnes, a worldly woman of high intelligence, immediately made friends with Rebecca. Before long, she learned of her ardent belief that Bula Matadi would lead them all to freedom someday. "He'll have to have the wit to do it... you teach him, Miss Agnes."

Miss Agnes, as she became known to all, was provided a private study where she began by teaching Madison his letters and later to read minor words. She often secretly wrote short stories, fairy tales, fables and nursery rhymes that she required him to read. Textbooks of any kind were forbidden; only the bible could serve as a primer. In spite of the restrictions, Madison steadily learned to read and write. Miss Agnes introduced Greek literature into his curriculum and by the time he was ten-years old, he had heard the most popular fables, understood that Aristotle was an advocate of personal freedom, and any slave who could read, write, and compute was a threat to the white man's dominance over them.

Madison loved reading and learning. He completed Genesis and Exodus by the fall of 1830, when he was eleven. He read aloud for Miss Agnes, the passages of Leviticus, Numbers, and Deuteronomy on his twelfth birthday. He learned to write excellent sentences and sometimes served as a scribe for Charles King, his mother and other slaves. When he was nearly a teenager, Miss Agnes recited all that she knew of William Shakespeare's, "The Merchant of Venice," requiring Madison to likewise memorize as much of it as he could.

"Who was Shylock?" Miss Agnes Quizzed.

Always eager to please his teacher, Madison was quick to answer. "A moneylender."

"And how was he viewed?"

"He was looked down upon because of his race."

"Why?"

"He was a Jew... they killed Christ—"

"And his reaction to these accusations?"

Without hesitation Madison answered, reciting

as if he were an actor upon a stage. "'I am a Jew,' said Shylock. 'Hath not a Jew eyes? Hath not a Jew hands, organs, dimensions, senses, affections, passions?'"

"Excellent!" Miss Agnes rushed from behind her desk and hugged him briefly, then held him at arm's length. "You must keep this knowledge to yourself, Madison. It will serve you well later in life. For now, just listen and learn and think."

Ruth King often stood at the door, listening. She shook her head but said nothing.

Madison developed early into a full-bodied teenager, strongly muscled and slim-waisted. His academic development raced along and at age fourteen, Miss Agnes tested him in his knowledge of science, mathematics, the arts, and worldly religions. "You have mastered all subjects beyond my best expectations, Madison. You have the mightiest of weapon of all. Do you know what that is?"

"Truth."

"And?"

"A knowledge of God."

Madison sat at his desk for a few moments, eyes closed, his hand resting on his chin. He suddenly closed his bible, rose from his chair, and placed his hands on his hips, as if he were the supreme authority addressing the Pharisees in the Temple of David. He stood before Miss Agnes, waiting, saying nothing.

Miss Agnes looked up from her own readings and beamed. *His moment of enlightenment has arrived.* "What is it, Madison?"

I was reading about the death of Jesus. I think that his life was much like Aristotle's."

"How?"

"In John's Gospel... I noticed how the Greek

philosopher and Jesus ... they did the same things."

"What things?"

"They gave up their lives for a cause. Everything they faced was all lies. They did not defend themselves."

"Why not?"

"Truth did not require explanation. It was supposed to be clear to their accusers. Do you agree?"

"No, I have a different opinion, but it doesn't matter."

"Why? What do you believe?"

"I ask the questions, Madison. But in this case I'll allow you to examine my point of view."

"Which is?"

"First, are you prepared to defend your position?"

"I am."

"Christ spoke Aramaic, a form of Hebrew. The prelate... Pontius Pilot... he spoke Latin. Perhaps Jesus was unable to reply to questions he did not understand."

"Miss Agnes! He was God... He understood everything!"

Miss Agnes' emerald eyes grew moist. After a lengthy pause, she replied. "I yield to your argument." She then quizzed him at length, finding great satisfaction in her pupil's ability to think freely and draw his own conclusions. "You amaze me young man. You may even fulfill your mother's dreams. In a way, with the knowledge you possess, you are already free. It is a treasure. Use it well."

Later that afternoon, Madison encountered Miss Agnes as she strode audaciously through the house. She collected a large tote bag near the front doors and left them swinging as she exited and descended the porch. An older driver held her buggy, and then helped her aboard. He handed her the reins. "God speed, Miss Agnes."

Madison, alarmed at her haste, followed on her heels.

"Where are you going, Miss Agnes—?"

"Bourbon Street."

"Why."

"I've got an itch."

"When will you be back?"

Miss Agnes' head bent low. She sighed and handed the reins to the driver. She slowly dismounted from the carriage and approached Madison. He was taller than her now, having matured into full manhood. "I am finished here. I won't be back."

"Please, Miss Agnes... why—?"

Miss Agnes met his eyes. "Madison, all of my life I have asked God, 'What have my people done to deserve this?' I've prayed for a liberator. I believe it is you. You have the keys to unlock us all."

"But I need you—"

"You need only yourself."

Miss Agnes then embraced him for the longest time, kissing him on both cheeks. "I love you, Bula Matadi. Do well." She remounted the buggy, clucked to her horse and snapped the reins. She did not look back as she sped through the tall oaks toward New Orleans.

Rebecca stood behind Madison, her hand rubbing the nape of his neck. "Dry your eyes, Son. She will always be with you."

Chapter Six

The Teenager

Madison was well mannered, polite and even-tempered. He behaved as Charles and Ruth King expected. Unconsciously, Charles took some delight in how Madison had developed and although denying it to others, he felt a genuine affection for him. From time to time, Charles took him along in the wagon to Woodville when he shopped for provisions. He showed Madison how to handle a team of horses and often handed him the reins. Later he taught Madison to ride and handle firearms.

On a crisp, cool fall morning, Madison carried the supplies for Charles King and his companions while they hunted Dove. Finally positioned around a freshly harvested field, Charles handed Madison a musket. "It's the newest creation... uses a percussion cap instead of the old flint and lock. The powder comes in a bag. This rifle would give a man the edge in a fight." He demonstrated the six steps to loading and handed the musket to Madison, telling him to take aim at a tree.

"Fire!" he commanded, and Madison pulled the

trigger, promptly falling backward onto his butt amid a cloud of smoke. Charles laughed and helped Madison to his feet. "It's like a mule, Madison; you handle it, don't let it handle you. Let's check your target." Charles put his arm around Madison's shoulder, leading him to inspect the tree. They were both amazed at the large hole in the center of it. "Good shootin', Boy."

Although Charles explained to his friends and church members that he was grooming Madison to become a Driver—a favored slave who would normally stand between the Master and the enslaved—he increasingly addressed him with terms of familiarity, if not outright endearment. Madison, mindful of Miss Agnes's cautions, did not exploit the intimacy. He always bowed his head, slumped his shoulders and replied, "Yes, Massa."

Within the mansion, Madison now read other important books. The prohibition on reading anything but the bible was never enforced. He perused several works of literature and delved into the classical writings of St. Augustine. Charles had handed the book to him one day as they rode a buggy to Woodville.

"Tell no one about this, Madison."

"Yes, Massa'"

"Be sure you understand me... I mean what I say, Son. They wouldn't understand."

Madison did as he was told, but secretly shared his views of humanity with the slaves, often holding them spellbound with his youthful oratory. Increasingly, he blended into slave society, feeling their suffering and addressing it with biblical or philosophical messages of hope. If they knew, Ruth and Charles never prohibited it, seemingly proud of Madison's intellectual growth.

Rufus Bohlinger complained that Madison was

inciting the slaves toward future disobedience, so Charles increased his wages and told him to overlook the boy. "He's Ruth's ticket to Heaven... leave him be."

Progressing through his teenage years, Madison spent more and more time among the slaves, sharing facts and knowledge he'd acquired from Miss Agnes. That he was one of them, he knew instinctively. Out of compassion for their plight, he often labored with them in the fields and helped with heavy chores around the slave quarters. He spent several evenings each week teaching young and old alike, how to read, make the letters of the alphabet and draw Arabic numbers. He was present at births and baptisms and worshiped with them when he could slip away at night. He became a favorite of the adult women. Teenage girls openly lusted for him, provoking much jealousy among the boys.

During a Fourth of July celebration, Madison competed in many of the games, winning a wood chopping contest and first-place in the gunnysack race. A bevy of admiring young girls encircled him as he saddled a stallion for the final contest: a horse race through backwoods of Kingland. Unaffected by the adulation, he waved his straw hat and rode to the start line.

"Hey, all," Madison greeted the other young competitors with a wide grin. He steadied his impatient steed like an expert. "Ya'all ready?"

Jenkins Longfellow, a burly young man nearly Madison's size, leered at him. "Ready ta' whup yo' ass. C'mon see what I has fer ya'." Jenkins nudged his Sorrel sidewise, pressing its flank against Madison's right leg.

Tobias Rathbone, another youthful rider, performed the same maneuver and pinned Madison's left leg against the horse. "Think you be Jesus himself, don't ya'?

What ya'all gonna' do now?"

Madison, unaccustomed to such hostility, sat speechless in the saddle. The starter raised his pistol. "Three... two... one... go!" He fired the starting shot.

Instantly, Madison wrapped one arm around the neck of Jenkins Longfellow and his other arm around Tobias Rathbone's neck, throwing them both to the ground. He dug his heels into the flanks of his mount, spurring the Roan forward at full gallop. The other riders were far ahead and Madison knew he had no chance to win this race. He reined up and allowed Jenkins and Thomas to come alongside of him. They dismounted and faced Madison.

"What was that all about? I thought we were friends." Madison said.

"We sick and tired a you comin' down from the big house like you sumpin' special... smart talk and all," Tobias said.

"All them girls wants is you," Jenkins whined. "Hell, been weeks since I had me a lady. Why don't you just stay up there with yo' white momma and yo' white daddy?"

A red-hot anger swelled in Madison's breast. "You just don't know about Miss Ruth and Charles. They took me and my momma in. Leave them out of this."

"See... you done turned white," Jenkins said." Now I'm gonna' teach you how it feels to get whupped real bad" He adopted a boxer's stance and balled his fists. He danced and jabbed the air toward Madison's face.

Madison prepared to defend himself. He spread his feet and raised his fists, his elbows locked at the waist. "Come on, now, do your best."

Jenkins telegraphed his first punch; a right cross. Madison caught his arm in the middle of the swing, bending it behind his back until his opponent fell to his knees begging for mercy. Jenkins' eyes flashed behind Madison and he turned in time to intercept Tobias racing toward him with a heavy tree limb. Madison sidestepped and caught the club as Tobias fell past him. In one blow he broke the thick branch across Tobias' back, laying him in the dirt of the trail. Approaching the two assailants, Madison placed his hands on his hips.

"Now look at you two worthless crybabies sitting on your butts. Why did you press me at the starting line?"

Neither boy replied. Fear of Madison held them on the ground.

"Come on, now... What do you have against me? Speak up!"

Tobias spoke first." See, there you go showin' off with them white words... like you be better than your brothers. You just don't fit in with us."

"My speech offends you?"

"It ain't all that," Jenkins said, rising from the ground and dusting himself off. "Ain't none of the girls hardly talk to us without throwin' you up to us. It's always "Madison this", and "Madison that.""

"I have something to say... I can't help what fortunes have come to me. Miss Agnes said I'm the bridge twixt Massa' Charles and our people. She wanted me to share what I know. I don't come down to the pens to steal the girls; I come to help my people."

"Help us? How you gonna' help us?" Tobias asked.

"I can teach you to read and write... learn the good news about Jesus. Now, I expect you two ignorant bucks to be at my Wednesday night bible studies. Agreed?"

Jenkins spoke slowly. "You say yo' kin teach me

to read? Teach me real writin'?"

"And you ain't havin' 'dem girls... for sure?" Tobias said. "Well, what time be the meetin'?"

Madison extended his hands, pulling Jenkins and Thomas to their feet. "No harm done. See you at sundown on Wednesday. Come out to the willow grove behind the big barn. Don't be late." With Jenkins and Tobias, Madison mentally counted fifteen pupils in his class. He'd soon have to add another evening to his schedule.

Chapter Seven

Deathbed Liberation

During the winter of 1837, when Madison was eighteen years old, Charles King contracted an illness, a flu-like sickness that ravaged his body and mind, bringing him to the threshold of death. He told Ruth that it seemed as if a demon had settled in his chest. He visited doctors in Natchez, and then New Orleans; none of whom could identify the illness or treat it. Out of desperation, he called upon Margarette, a well-known healer and part-time practitioner of the black arts, residing near Jackson, Louisiana.

Margarette sat in a flimsy rocker, gnawing and puffing on a long-stemmed corncob pipe. Her weathered face remained passive as two of his Negro servants carried Charles into the weather beaten old shack on a pallet.

"Lay him 'cross them sea trunks... there by the wall," Margarette ordered. "I'll need to study him a bit."

Charles, drugged with opium and nearly delirious, hardly noticed his surroundings except for the odor of incense, mixed with magnolia, rosemary, and other aromatic plants. Charles gagged and bawled, "What is that

God-awful smell? I'm dead... 'tis the stench of Hades."

Ruth surveyed the dimly lit room, taking into account the many exotic artifacts adorning the shelves and walls. Red, blue, and green ceramic vases littered the floor. Multicolored small decorative tiles hung from the ceiling, intermingled with beads and imitation jewelry. Several dozen oils, watercolors, inks, and prints of odd-looking creatures were haphazardly mounted to the walls. Numerous sculptures and wooden images sat amid pottery shards—Zemi idols, and stone tools—all crowding the shelves of this dilapidated cabin. Ruth was counting flint blades amid the debris when she drew back. In one corner sat a small dugout filled with human skulls and bones. A fat rodent scurried across the floor.

"Good God, Woman... From where did you originate? Are you a witch... some sort of voodoo queen?"

"I am an Amerindian goddess of the rain forest."

"Africa?"

"Malliouhana, in Anquilla."

"Where, pray tell, is that?"

"Caribbean."

Charles struggled to sit up on his cot. "Good Lord, woman... Just shut up and tend to me. I'm dying." He coughed spasmodically and fell back onto the bed.

Margarette was a direct descendent of an ancient Indian culture. She had arrived in America as a refugee from a storm-grounded sailing vessel. First working the bars and hotel lobbies of New Orleans, she plied a living reading Tarot cards and telling fortunes. Later she found the tourists more appreciative of her natural, albeit un-common cures for hangovers, stomach ulcers and several varieties of venereal diseases. One wealthy baroness from Selma, Alabama, brought her preteen son, afflicted with uncontrollable bed-wetting, to Margarette. She promptly cured him with several doses of a brew made from the poisonous oleander plant, skunk glands, garlic and other herbs. So grateful was the baroness, she bestowed upon Margarette a small fortune and her fame spread throughout the south. Practicing her unusual trade without license, a constable's investigation caused her to flee to the back-woods of Jackson, just a few miles north of Baton Rouge.

"Can you help us," Ruth asked.

"Ah see. Maybe I kin... maybe I kin't."

Margarette sprung from her rocker like a coiled snake, circling her patient several times. Finally she stopped at Charles' head, touched it for a moment, and then pried open his eyelids, staring into the sockets.

"Loose up his bed shirt," she told Ruth.

Margarette placed her ear against Charles' chest, listening intently to the moist rasp. "Ah seed' me a case like this once 'afore," the weathered old hag announced. "Draw me some o' his water. Ah makes sure."

Ruth was appalled. "Do you mean his urine? That's disgusting. How can I—"

"Please, please, Ruth, I'll do as she says. Give me a glass," Charles demanded.

Ruth selected a dull-colored wide-brimmed jar from a shelf and gave it to Charles. He promptly went beneath the covers and emerged a moment later with an ounce or more of urine. Ruth handed it to Margarette. "Here. What can you possibly surmise from this?"

Margarette dipped her finger into the yellow liquid, raised it to her nose and sniffed it several times. She smiled at Ruth, and then suddenly lifted the glass to her lips, filling her mouth with the foul smelling waste. Her cheeks puffed in and out as she rinsed it through her teeth.

She gagged, and then spat it into a vase. "Consumption," she announced after a few moments.

"Consumption," Ruth repeated. "My God, are you certain?"

"Consumption," Charles groaned. I'm doomed."

"Can you do anything for him?" Ruth asked.

Margarette sat down in her rocker, drew hard on her pipe until it was sufficiently stoked, and replied: "Ain't be but one... maybe two things kin fix this."

"What things, what cures?" Ruth asked.

"Ah' fix him a tonic," Margarette said after some pause. "Might work." She fed Charles several red peppers and a strong brew made from sassafras roots, red sage, jimson weed and other herbs. In a few minutes his eyesight dimmed and he cried out for water. Soon thereafter, his nose began to bleed. Charles sat up and clutched his chest. He moaned, and then coughed violently, spitting wads of blood into a wooden bucket. Margarette shook her head.

"Umm, 'it ain't takin'. Ya'all might has to use number two."

"And what, pray tell, is that?" Ruth asked. She had tried to dissuade Charles from seeing this witch, believing it blasphemed the Lord.

"I needs my three dollars, first. I doesn't work for free," Margarette said.

"Pay the woman!" Charles insisted.

Ruth pulled several bills from her purse and handed them to Margarette. "Now, woman... what will restore his health?"

"Put yo' man in the wagon... take him to the house. Carve out his stone."

Charles passed out. Ruth shrieked: "You said you had a second cure!"

"There ain't no cure. I said there was jus' two things kin fix this. First one didn't work. The other one will."

"There is nothing... not a thing that you know of that will help?"

Margarette puffed a few times, removed the pipe from her mouth and said, "Well, there be one thing you might could try."

"What is it?" Ruth demanded to know.

Margarette offered Ruth a clean, but well-worn white cloth, claiming it had touched the hem of Jesus' robe and had been handed down to her. "It been known ta' work miracles," she said. "Two dollars."

Charles wasted away in his bed for several weeks with his family and household servants around him. Before he grew too weak, he called Ruth to his bedside. "Let Madison have his freedom," he whispered out his order. "Turn loose any of the others that you choose. I've seen the Angel Gabriel. Jesus was by his side; He's coming for me. I'm ready to meet him. This unholy convention, this slaving... it's sinful. Save your soul, Ruth. Emancipate them all."

In a few days, Charles King drew his last breath and died. He was buried in a graveyard at Natchez, along the banks of the Mississippi River. Throngs of friends and business acquaintances gathered there, along with many of his slaves. Madison and Rebecca were among them. Upon their return to Woodville, they learned that the word of their impending freedom had spread. Around the fires that night a memorial service was held for Charles King and his slaves called him a good man. Somber African rhythms were beat out on hollow log drums and mournful wailing echoed across the fields.

"The weeping may be more for what will happen to us, not for Charles King," Rebecca told Madison. "I'm worried."

"Don't be worried, Momma. Like the Israelites, God is leading our people out of bondage. Everything will be all right."

Rufus Bohlinger and his husky foreman, Coley Thompson, sat atop horses, on a hilltop, watching the slaves in their mourning. After a while, he spat tobacco juice, whipped his horse along the flanks, and with Coley, they rode off into the night. "Damn Niggras think they going free, do they? Well, I got something to say about that."

Chapter Eight

Chains Done Broke At Last

It was hot and steamy southern afternoon, about a week after Charles King's death, when Ruth held an assembly of all the slaves from the front porch of her mansion. When summoned, they moved hastily to the gathering point—understanding the purpose and importance of the meeting. On the veranda of this great southern manor, Ruth King stood side by side with Rebecca and Madison.

Young and old, healthy and frail, the many slaves of Charles King gathered in a semicircle, facing Ruth. Some had lived on the King plantation all of their lives. Another couple had arrived only a month before. They stood together as families and as friends. Fathers carried their young children on their shoulders. Mothers held up their babies and moved them in an arc, showing them the long-prohibited areas of the white Massa's holdings and the woman who would now unlock their chains.

Their mood was jovial; their confidence in the impending liberation a sure thing. Rebecca and Madison were a part of why they were being freed and they, above all, were to be trusted.

Jacob Smallwood, almost eighty years old, lifted his cane and pointed at the mansion. He remarked that he had laid the footings and supervised the installation of the massive white columns. "Massa's daddy... he leave me be after that."

"I forged and hammered that iron back in twenty-five," Lucius Gains, another older man replied. He pointed toward the beautiful wrought iron framework on the second floor balcony. "I was three years forging those windows."

"Freedom... 'bout to come now," Jacob said.

An atmosphere of joy enveloped the slave assemblage and took on an energy all its own. A gentle slow humming began in the rear of the multitude, and then swelled and rolled rapidly over them. Rhythmic hand clapping erupted and suddenly a cantor shouted praises to God. A tall, bewhiskered, white-haired man stepped forward, raised his arms to summon attention, and then directed his congregation in songs of bliss and rapture.

Jerimiah Kelly, a slave of twenty years and the father of three daughters, embraced the oldest, Nakira. "Every so often I'm kinda' sorry for bringing you children into this world. You'll have your freedom now... freedom to dream."

Nakira, a strikingly beautiful teenager, smiled and grasped her sister Gesenda's hand. "Won't fritter it away, Daddy." She clapped her hands and began rocking to the rhythms of the spirited songs.

Intuitively, groups of slaves formed in separate rings of ten to twenty: dancing, stamping their feet and shouting. Gradually they merged together, creating a single large circle. They shouted long forbidden spirituals—melodies crafted over the years at clandestine nighttime prayer meetings in the barns and stables of the plantation. In perfect harmony, one hundred and twenty-two voices sang.

> "Jordan River, I'm bound to go,
> Bound to go, bound to go,
> Jordan River, I'm bound to go,
> And bid 'em fare ye' well.
> My Brudder Robert, I'm bound to go,
> Bound to go, Bound to go.
> My Sister Lucy, I'm bound to go,
> Bound to go, Bound to go."

The huge human ring began to sway, first clock-wise, then counter clockwise, moving slowly at first, and then with an ever-quickening pace. The jubilant slaves sang and shouted their melodic phrases over and over, producing an ecstatic state among the singers. Several women screamed and fell. Dancing men and boys stepped out of the ring, exhausted.

Ruth King haltingly edged her way down from the porch, walked across the yard and stood near the outer circle. Overcome by the hypnotic movements of the crowd, she joined in, smiling and clapping her hands.

"You got it now, Miss Ruth," a cheerful Rebecca called out to her. "Bend yo' knee... raise yo' hip... put yo' hands together... One N' two, N' one N' two. That's it, Miss Ruth!"

The singing reverberated across the hills and grain fields, stirring animals in their stalls and scowling overseers on horseback. Tears filled Ruth King's eyes and she shouted to God to take her home. She felt closer to Him at this moment than she had ever been in her life. Song after song filed the air and Ruth, euphoric with emotion, was incapable of stopping it.

"These are God's people, Charles... you were right to free them." Ruth tried to repeat the words of a song but lost it in the roar of celebration.

A banjo and fiddle appeared in the throng of black faces. In rhythm with their tinny reverberations, a simple, but fundamental song burst through:

"Slavery chain done broke at last,
Broke at last, broke at last,
Slavery chain done broke at last,
Going to praise God till I die..."

The festival of freedom lasted for nearly an hour when Rebecca finally took Ruth by the arm. "This could go on forever, Miss Ruth. Tell me when you want to stop it and make your announcement."

"I suppose you're right, I should get on with it. I wish Charles were here."

Rebecca nodded to Madison. He raised his arms for several moments, then waved back and forth, demanding silence. "Hey! Hey, ya'all!" He shouted. "Please... Please! Miss Ruth has something to say."

The slaves nudged each other and asked for quiet. A hush fell over the crowd and all eyes focused on Ruth: Their moment had arrived.

Ruth took notice of several mounted overseers in the rear. They shifted their restless horses back and forth along the fringes of the crowd. "You are dismissed, gentlemen," she called out. "It is not necessary that you remain for the content of my message. Rufus will inform you later. Please depart now!"

The horsemen backed away, slowly, eyeing the crowd. Rufus Bohlinger was nowhere to be found. He was in Woodville, holding a meeting of his own.

Rebecca, now Ruth's most trusted confident, held a large leather pouch. Ruth cleared her throat and began: "In the name of the Lord Almighty and in the memory of my dear husband Charles, I am announcing his final desires. You have been faithful and good servants to Charles and me. As we grew to know each other, we grew fond of you people."

A murmur rose from the crowd. "You people?" Nakira Kelly remarked.

Ruth heard, but could not tell if the comment projected approval or discontent. She hurried along. "You all know that Rebecca and Madison have fared well, living in our home. Why, he can read and work his numbers. Now you will have your freedom too, and with God's protection and mercy, you will be able to do the same. In this pouch are the legal papers guaranteeing manumission for you all."

"What the hallelujah does that mean?" Lucius Gains asked.

Jacob Smallwood laughed. "It means we been set free; we ain't no slaves no mo'."

"Then why don't she just say we been set free?"

"In a way, that's what she did say. See, when a Massa' set a slave loose, he worry about it during the night. He sorta' wish he hadn't. Next mornin' he look around in the pens and say "Where's my man Lucius…? Then he hit his-self and say, "Oh, man-you-missin'."" Jacob slapped himself on the knee, bursting with laughter. Lucius stared at him in disbelief, but did offer a faint smile after a bit.

Rebecca held the heavy pouch above her head and moved it in an arc before the crowd. A murmur of approval rose from the lips of the elders. Hand clapping and shouts interrupted Ruth. Madison raised his arms high above his head, asking for silence.

"Madison will call out your names... your family names. Come forward and receive your certificates," Ruth announced. "I wish that you would all stay on... remain at Kingland with me. Those of you that choose to do so will receive acreage... fair wages—"

Ruth could not finish. The slaves began another ecstatic uproar of song and shouts. Hats and small children tumbled into the air. Someone fired a musket but it frightened no one. More shots rang out as part of the celebration. It took several minutes before Madison could begin reading the names. The former chattels of Ruth and Charles King, now free, approached her, bowing slightly or nodding. Some hugged her, others touched her hand, and still others simply took their documents and backed away. Grown men wiped away tears and uttered their thanks. Dozens more promised that they would remain and work the land in return for a plot of fertile land or wages. A group of young girls and their mothers planned a thanksgiving festival for later that evening. Men clutched their certificates, stared at them, and then handed the legal documents to Madison to read and explain.

"What does it say?" an old man asked.

"It says you are free, Sir. Free as the eagle!"

Madison read every certificate for every former slave. Nodding their understanding, men and women, hugging one another, ambled back to their cabins where they slaughtered pigs and chickens and prepared for the celebration. Young boys gathered firewood and old men found their liquor stock. Ancient African songs of praise and joy filled the air and children danced around the cooking fires.

In one circle, however; several men voiced their displeasure at the whole affair; and their misgivings about their newly bestowed liberation. They sat on tree stumps or on the earth, gathered around an influential elder.

King David, a sinewy middle-aged man, offered that, "all whites are wicked... made by the devil himself."

"But they set us free," one lad argued.

"You watch... see if that bastard Rufus don't make a mess of it."

Several men nodded their heads.

King David continued: "She never said they was sorry for what they done to us. I waited to hear it, but she play like she doing us some kinda' good turn,"

Billy Sampson, an older man, agreed. Inherently defiant, Billy had been born into slavery in Virginia, sold at auction several times and had never buckled under the harsh treatment of ruthless overseers. At Kingland, he had been whipped repeatedly for failed escape attempts and "propagating agitation," as Rufus explained the whippings to Charles King.

"Well, what we going to do? We tell her we don't want no papers?" a young man asked. "Possum in the hand be better than two coon up a tree."

"Don't know about ya'all," King David replied, but me, I'm headed north in the morning... get gone out of here 'afore Rufus upset the whole applecart."

"I hear Texas is a good place," Billy said.

"Don't you believe it," King David shouted. He stood and threw down a small twig he had been chewing. "Ain't no place in this whole United States be good for us... go north to Canadee."

Madison noticed these few malcontents, separated as they were from the bustling colony of former slaves. He approached them and listened for a while, then offered: "Miss Ruth will keep her word. Are you willing to give up the land she promised, the wages?"

Billy Sampson scowled at Madison. "Where we gonna' spend it?" How we gonna' buy seed... tools? No Woodville storekeeper ever gonna' let us in the door. They ain't so much as gonna' touch our hand… or our money. They ain't gonna' just stand by and let us blossom out."

"Suit yourselves, my friends, but here you have a chance to make something for your children. God is good." Madison retorted.

"Yeah, God be good, but that Rufus Bohlinger been overlooked by the Almighty," King David argued. "You stay, he'll wipe you all out. I'm for getting off this place right quick."

The malcontents continued their debate throughout the late afternoon, weighing the possibilities of starting new lives in distant lands or remaining at Kingland and trusting that Ruth King would fulfill her promises. Several men vowed to leave in the morning; others concluded that it was best to remain.

Rufus Bohlinger, a tall man with perpetual anger etched on his face, finished his conversations with the prominent men of Woodville. He shook hands with the sheriff and started for the door of the town hall. "It's agreed then; we keep them Niggras in their place. Come midnight, ya'all have your boys meet me at the tall oaks behind the big house." He slammed the door on his way out.

The night sky glowed red from the many cooking fires burning throughout the lodgings. Wood smoke lay low across the fields, and as the temperature cooled, it gave the appearance of clouds hugging the earth. Occasional gunshots interrupted the song and dance. Children played tag in the flickering firelight and young lovers slipped off through the shadows. Stringed instruments and drums added to the festive mood. Older folks held a prayer meeting and thanked the Lord for his blessings.

"Jesus say he be comin' on a cloud," Reverend Carter, their resident preacher observed. "If this ain't it, it's mighty close to it. Ya'all reach up and grab a holt' to the hand of Jesus."

"Hold on," the crowd shouted. "Hold on..."

At some point in the service, Reverend Carter took over as cantor. His chant rose slowly from his soul, eventually reaching a fever pitch as he called on God to guide and bless them. Sweat poured from his brow and he broke into a dance, a rhythmic shuffle, straight out of Africa. His words praised the Lord for His generosity and wisdom and he pleaded for His merciful embrace of all Africans, past and present. With measured cadence and his voice throbbing with weighty elocution, his words moved his audience into a hypnotic state. They echoed his every petition: "Oh, Jesus! Oh, Jesus! You have slain... You brought down.... You whupped the evil one. Oh yes, Jesus, you saved our people. Oh my Jesus—"

"Oh Jesus, Yes, Jesus!" The crowd responded, leaping and thrusting their hands into the night sky.

"Almighty God, Oh, my God, you blesses us with water, you clothe our naked bodies, you feed our hungry, and now you set me free, Oh, my God..."

"I am free... my God has made us free! Free! Free!"

Totally absorbed with the rituals, Ruth King watched from her rocker on the porch. Rebecca stood beside her, anxious to go to the pens and join in the celebrations. From time to time, she echoed the words of the cantor. "Oh, my Jesus... thank you, Jesus..."

Madison was overwhelmed by the jubilation

pouring forth from his people. An unexpected wave of
emotion passed through him. He grabbed his mother tightly
by the waist, and then reached for Ruth.

"Bless you," he said and squeezed her hand.

"They have muskets?" Ruth asked."

Madison laughed. "Oh, they have a lot of secrets,
but there's no need to worry now... that's all over"

"What is the Cantor saying? He is so passionate."

"Yes, Miss Ruth," Rebecca answered. He's calling on the Lord... giving thanks and praying for a rich
and blessed future in Heaven. He uses the rhythms of our
homeland."

"I could jump up and walk on those words,"
Madison said. "He moves my soul."

Ruth turned toward Rebecca and Madison.
"Charles cared deeply for you, Maddy. He couldn't show
it, but he was proud of you. Go join your people... both
of you."

"You'll be all right?" Rebecca asked.

"Yes. Go on now, celebrate the night and celebrate your freedom. I'll be fine."

Madison and Rebecca walked quickly toward
the bonfires. They began skipping, and then dancing as
they drew closer. Rebecca clapped her hands, hugged her
friends, cried and shouted, "Praise Jesus ... it's all good!"

Madison filled a tin plate of food for his mother
and himself. He sat quietly on a log, eating and watching
the celebrants and feeling good inside.

Rufus Bohlinger, from within the shadows of
hundred-year-old oaks, mounted his horse. "I hear riders
coming, Mr. Thompson. Got your torch?" He checked his
pistol. The action worked well and he had plenty of ammo.

Chapter Nine

The Road to Natchez

The hoof beats of many riders came nearer and nearer, finally stopping in front of Rufus. He moved his horse from under the trees and faced them. Words were unnecessary; the plan was well known. With a nod from Rufus, they lit their torches, pulled their pistols, muskets, and whips, and then followed his charge through the thicket, across the fields and straight into the campfires of the celebrating families.

Screams of terror shattered the sounds of joyous triumph and clapping hands as Rufus and his nightriders plunged into the throngs. Galloping recklessly up and down and between the cabins, they trampled several terror-filled men and women. They threw their torches into and atop the dwellings, setting them ablaze. Some marauders fired their muskets and pistols into the air; others found their mark and lead balls slammed into the body of a child and an old man.

Ashley Smallwood, Jacob's fifteen year old granddaughter, broke free from her young lover's arms at the first sign of trouble and fled into the cornfields. Exhausted, she fell beneath the hoof beats of a torch-bearing white fanatic. The rider reined up, dismounted and knelt beside her quivering body. She looked up at him, her olive eyes pleading for mercy. He slapped her hard, and then ripped her clothing, exposing her supple breasts. Aroused by the exquisite form of her upper body, he shredded her dress completely, slowly examining her with his torch. Filled with uncontrollable lust at the sight of her naked figure, he ravaged her mercilessly, squeezing her neck as he rode her up and down. Somewhere during the evil act, life passed from Ashley. The villain rolled her body over with the toe of his boot. He then mounted his horse and returned to the fires.

"Ya'all catch ya' any Niggras, Rufus?" A raider shouted.

"Just one... she ain't complaining."

King David, Billy Sampson and several others recognized Rufus when the riders first approached. They took off at a dead run into the fields but pursuing horsemen quickly surrounded them, firing pistol shots into the air. They herded the escapees in a tight ball of humanity, making them kneel and plead for their lives.

"What we have here?" An approaching rider demanded to know.

"Damn your evil soul, Rufus Bohlinger," King David fearlessly shouted at the man. You'll twist forever in the fires of hell!"

"You go first, Niggra," Rufus calmly remarked, pointing his pistol at King David. "I been wantin' to get rid o' your uppity black ass since I first laid eyes on you."

King David saw his impending death. His chest swelled, he put his hands on his hips and spat a wad of mucus directly in front of Rufus' feet. "Go to hell!"

Rufus immediately pulled the trigger, sending a ball deep into the forehead of his antagonist. King David slumped and died instantly, his freedom having lasted less than twenty-four hours. Rufus and his raiders herded the others back to the pens.

There, amid the agonizing, howling chaos, Madison spotted his mother, her arms held behind her by a hooded nightrider. Another man unbuckled his pants, forcing her to the ground. Holding his stiff member in one hand, the rapist went unconscious from the large rock Madison slammed into his head. A rifle stock smashed across Madison's skull and he felt the sting of a whip for the first time in his life. He fell into an unconscious heap.

The carnage continued for several hours; the former slaves unable to offer any resistance. In the light of the burning houses, Rufus ordered riders into the fields to run down and capture those who had escaped.

In the morning, amid the gray smoke and ashes of their homes, the slaves sat silently, in family groups, in shock—most of them with their hands bound behind their backs. The stench of death and burning cinders lay in a low cloud over the pens. Women and children sobbed softly and the men made whispered promises of escape— revenge at the very least. Several boys, obeying the orders of their fathers, delivered water from wooden buckets to the stunned slaves, which they drank and used to bathe their wounds.

Rufus Bohlinger rode among them, cracking his whip above their heads and shouting orders. His posse was unmasked now and they were drunk with the power that comes to savages when they lord over other men. "Ya'all Niggras ain't staying here. You ain't getting no land and you can forget them notions 'bout freedom. Things gonna' stay the same. Try to outsmart me... you run... I'll track you down. I'll kill ya' where ya' stand. Charles King is gone now and you belong to me. You are my slaves... I am your Massa'!"

Too frightened and too bewildered to protest, the captives sat in small groups, silent, hugging one another. The joy of that brief moment of freedom now gone from their hearts; it was but an instant of liberty. "I knew it wasn't true," one slave observed.

No one dared to ask Rufus his motivation or his intentions. In his sadistic euphoria, rooted in the power he wielded over the slaves, he was bloodthirsty and dangerous. Sitting atop his dappled horse, he fumed like a King Herod, raging insult and abuse upon his subjects. To validate his absolute rule over the slaves and prove that he was now the master of their destiny, he announced his plans: "Ya'all be going up to Natchez... Forks of the Road. Ya'all be put up for sale. Any Niggra... any man, woman or child who defies me will taste my whip. Now git up! We're moving. Get up, I say!"

Slowly, the slaves stood, helping each other and calling out to their confused children. They got in line, two by two, as Rufus instructed them to do.

Madison held his hand over his bloody head wound. He looked for his mother, Rebecca, and found her bruised and battered, her clothes shredded, sitting near the hot ashes of the home where Isaac had lived. She did not cry; she was beyond tears.

Madison hands were not bound. Unnoticed by the raiders, he lay all night in a semiconscious state. He helped his mother to her feet and untied her. "I saved our papers, Momma. Everything will be all right."

Rufus and his men rode among the slaves, forming them into a long column. At his command, the grueling march to Natchez began.

"God help us," Rebecca said. She turned and saw Ruth King standing on her porch waving meekly. Rebecca didn't wave back.

"God's not listening right now, Momma."

It was a three-day journey up the seventy-five mile road to Natchez. Under a blazing sun, the parade of dispirited prisoners shuffled along the dusty, rutted wagon trail that first day. Some held hands while others helped the weak, the elderly and the children. They made camp alongside the road late in the evening. A summer thunderstorm erupted, blasting them with cold torrential rains. Without shelter and denied permission to seek any, they huddled together for warmth and comfort. No one called out to the Lord or begged for mercy. They were beyond all spiritual hope and devoid of any thoughts for deliverance.

At daybreak on the second day the rains stopped and by ten o'clock in the morning the sun cooked the earth and seared the backs of the slaves as they trudged ever northward. Rufus Bohlinger and his men rode their horses up and down the line of confused and weary marchers, often laying their whips square on the back of a man or woman or child when they took the notion to do so. The hired hands, inspired by Rufus Bohlinger's cruel example of oppression, took the time to beat, rape and otherwise dehumanize individual slaves when the impulse struck.

When a slave faltered, others picked them up and carried them, quietly urging them to "hold on." Jacob Smallwood died from exhaustion. Tobias Rathbone and Jenkins Longfellow fled toward the forest late in the afternoon of the second day, but were recaptured quickly. Rufus supervised the savage beatings each of them received. Tobias bled to death within a few hours. The marauders discarded his body a few feet off the road, scantily covering him with leaves and shrubbery. Jacob Smallwood was left exposed beneath the searing sun. Reverend Carter prayed briefly for each soul as he walked. He was forbidden to stop and conduct a service.

Rebecca began to weaken late that day and at times Madison carried her. When they rested, he prayed incessantly; it was all he could offer to sustain her. "Don't give up, Momma... hold on. We'll be free again." Madison said, drawing her close to him.

Near the end of the day, the entourage of broken humanity fell alongside the shoulders of the road, exhausted, thirsty, and starving. About dusk, a small band of slaves from nearby farms and plantations came along the road offering water, food and comfort to their brothers and sisters. Rufus Bohlinger and his men sat by and watched as the Samaritans untied the hands of the bound prisoners and fed them.

"They lettin' 'em loose," Coley Thompson said. "You gonna' allow that, Rufus?"

"There ain't no problem now, Mr. Thompson; we got 'em broke.... They don't know which way to run. You see one tryin' to scoot, just shoot 'em."

Madison stayed close to his mother, assuring her they'd present their certificates and be freed at Natchez. He took her wrists and arms in his big hands and massaged them to improve the circulation. An older black man stopped by, giving them water, pork skins, and fresh biscuits. He sat beside Rebecca and Madison, hands folded in prayer, but whispering something else.

"Ah be Amos Jefferson," he said. "We from da'

Rhoades plan'ashun. Keep faith... listen ta' me, now."

Madison studied the man's face. He seemed to be sure of himself and was clearly the supervisor of the relief workers.

Amos opened one finger of his folded hands and pointed east. "If ya'all kin slip away, come back ta' that farm over yonder." He said quietly. "We has a fair Massa'. He send us out with these victuals. You don't wanna' nev'a get to the forks."

"Thank you," Rebecca said. "We are free... We have papers—"

"You hits the forks, them papers hain't good fer nothin'. Land sakes, woman... you is in Mizzippi!"

"We'll be fine, Sir. Thank you. Mrs. King will come fetch us."

"God's mercy on you, Sister... your boy, too." He moved on to attend other prisoners. He circulated without hesitation among the slaves doing what he could to encourage them. He showed no fear of Rufus Bohlinger.

During the third day, several more men died under the whip. A few expired from weariness and others simply gave up. Rufus Bohlinger and his men took great pleasure in the misery of their captives. They raped at will, sometimes in the open, deflowering young girls hardly old enough to understand what was happening to them. Madison watched, building a lifelong hatred for white men and he vowed to avenge his people someday. B*reaker of Stones you named me, Momma. I'll crush these stones on the rock of the Lord's altar.*

It was high noon on the third day when the trail of broken bodies stumbled their way through the dusty streets of Natchez, a riverboat community along the Mississippi. Town folk stayed shuttered in their houses—

Rufus Bohlinger's reputation for violence having preceded him—and the belief that all slaves emanated disease.

Not far from the eastern limits of the city, about a mile, they came upon a large open field. The roads divided there. Liberty road went east and then southeast toward southern Alabama and Georgia. Old Courthouse Road led northeast into Alabama and Tennessee. They had reached their destination: Forks of the Road. It was a collection of rough and primitive buildings sitting directly in the angle made by the roads.

Rebecca had barely survived the march. She fell prostrate on a bed of grass, exhausted and discouraged. Madison stood guard over his mother. "We're here, Momma. I'll find some water. You'll be all right."

Of the multitude of King Plantation slaves who had experienced a few hours of freedom, only one-hundred and eight made it to the slave pens at the Forks of the Road.

Chapter Ten

The Forks of The Road

Rufus Bohlinger halted the march when he was about a hundred yards from the Forks in the Road. "Ya'all keep an eye on 'em," he shouted to his men. He spurred his horse forward toward the cluster of ramshackle buildings. His weary captives fell in heaps alongside the road.

"Hey all!" Rufus shouted. "I brought a coffle of slaves up from Woodville. Where's Bankston... man what runs this place?" Without waiting for a reply, Rufus goaded his horse forward, trotting boldly through a wide gate and deeper into the camp.

Madison sat at the edge of a ditch with his arm around Rebecca. He fed her a few salty chicken gizzards, crackers and water from the ration gifts of the second day. Others sat in family groups, most of them appearing to be either asleep or having fainted. He watched the forward progress of Rufus Bohlinger, vowing to kill him someday. *I'll give our papers to this man called Bankston... then I'll take my mother home.*

The Forks of the Road was a cluster of about forty shabby, long, low buildings. Pine shingles covered some roofs, others were made of tin. A few well-built log houses fenced the outer perimeter. They were more permanent in construction and somewhat stylish; obviously the headquarters buildings. Behind them the shacks were more weather-beaten and dilapidated. Smoke rose from the chimneys but no workers appeared in the gardens and fields beyond. The entire perimeter of the compound was fenced with a three-rail, split-log barrier.

In the front courtyard, a group of Negroes gathered in a semicircle. Madison counted about eight of them. They were all dressed the same, with course corduroy velvet trousers, white cotton shirts, black vests, and wearing round furry caps, centered on their heads. Their fashionable and shiny black shoes were not made for field work, but were nonetheless, sturdy. Several white men were passing from one slave to another, inspecting them. Four tall boys, dressed in the same uniform, stood at the corners of the largest building, as if they were military guards. Rufus neared the steps of the log building and two of the boys ran forward, taking the reins of his horse and bowing slightly as they did so.

"Massa' Bankston inside, Suh." One of the boys said. "He told us ta' fetch ya'."

Rufus dismounted and released the horse to one of the lads. "Feed and water him... curry comb, too. We've had a hard three days."

"Yes, Suh."

Rufus walked briskly up the porch steps and pushed his way inside the main house. A portly red-faced man sat behind an opulent mahogany desk, examining several open ledgers. Dressed in a white cotton suit of a southern businessman, he presented an air of authority simply by sitting there. Without looking up, he said,

"You're Rufus... Charles King's man. I heard about you and that burning you done, Piker."

Rufus was unperturbed by the remark. He had haggled with slave traders before. Buyers and sellers permitted no advantage to one another, always vying for bargaining position through insults and intimidation.

Rufus surveyed the room. It was lavishly furnished with antiques, dressers and a huge wooden cabinet that held muskets and modern rifles. A large Persian rug covered most of the oak floor. Several closed doorways led to rooms that Rufus assumed were living quarters. *I'd say this son of a bitch is rich. Play my cards right and I'll come away with some sizable profit.*

He strode forward, leaned his fists on the desk and faced the little fat man. "I'm the law down at King's place. I torched them pens to kill any disease... clean it up. Charles died, and his missus... well, she done gone soft in the head. Charles turned it all over to me 'afore he passed on.

Bankston focused on his ledgers, rolling a feathered pen between his fingers. "You sure about that? I heard different. I heard Ruth was keeping' the place... freed her Negroes—"

"I been the head man at Kingland nigh on ten years. I'm selling off the place: the Niggras, the cattle... everything. I'm sending Ruth up to her kin in Ohio. She approved of all that."

Isaac Bankston had been a slave merchant for thirty-years. In collaboration with John Armstead, they were the most active flesh traders in the United States. Armstead served as a traveling purchaser in Virginia, scouring slave holding pens for his merchandise. They maintained a set of offices in sight of the nation's capital where men argued loudly each day about liberty and independence; but none of that mattered to Isaac Bankston and John Armstead. They had grown rich, buying and selling human beings, without regard for any notions of liberty.

In Virginia, where the slave population exceeded that of all other states, John Armstead bought at prices much cheaper than the sale price of slaves in the deep south. After assembling a group of a hundred or more slaves, they were marched overland to Mississippi, manacled together. The women, sometimes unshackled, carried their small children on their backs while the older siblings walked beside them. The men, often beaten for their slow pace or outbursts of soulful murmurings and prayer, remained chained together. They were forbidden to speak to, or mingle with their wives and children.

The march continued day and night, with little rest, except when a slave stumbled, too weak to continue. There was no shelter, and provisions were meager at best. Slave women foraged in the brush or fields for grain, berries, and nuts. Occasionally a rabbit or a squirrel might be snared or stunned by a well-aimed stone. The raw meat was distributed amongst families, who near starvation, swallowed their allotment whole.

White farmers sometimes came down from their fields as the train of human misery passed, selling dried beef, pork and corn—thereby profiting from the misery of the slaves. More often, a young lad, an attractive teenage girl, or a few small children were taken as payment for the food and water. Mounted horseman, armed with guns and whips, supervised the long march and every aspect of their journey. Those slaves who expired along the way were buried in unmarked plots, their memories left to the shifting sands of history.

Their route took them through the Cumberland Gap, across the Appalachians, and then southward into Tennessee. After a few days rest near Memphis, they proceeded on to northern Mississippi, taking the Natchez trace down to the Forks of the Road. The entire journey took six weeks or more. It was trail of tears and battered humanity.

Armstead often accompanied the coffles on their way south. He viewed the slaves as objects, not worthy of pity or consideration. When business was good and slaves were needed quickly, Bankston and Armstead transported their cargoes to the New Orleans market by ship, rather than march them overland. It was more expensive, but as with any commodity, supply and demand determined the final price. Loaded aboard one of the several slave brigs of the day, the slaves sailed past the southern tip of Florida, and then across the gulf, arriving at New Orleans a little more than a week after having left Virginia. Occasionally they walked to their final destinations, but often, steam brigs brought them up the Mississippi River to Natchez, depositing them near the gates of this elaborate slave market.

Isaac Bankston knew a thieving liar when he saw one. Remaining seated, he laid down his feather pen, closed his ledger and evaluated Rufus. "How many you bring? What kinda' shape they in? Any fever?"

"Why, they're in good condition... lived right well at the King place. I got more than a hundred head standin' across the road,"

Isaac Bankston rose, placed his fists on his desk, leaned forward and glared into Rufus's face.

"What skills? Any female mulattoes...?"

"Yes... most is healthy... strong. There's carpenters, masons, weavers, iron smithies... about any trade you'd want. Couple a fair women—"

"You mark 'em up any... whipped 'em? Mistreated slaves don't market too good. My buyers don't shell out money for an unruly slave."

Rufus was unprepared for Isaac Bankston's aggressive questioning. He realized he would have to speak more forcefully if he were to stay in control of the negotiations. "Damn it, Mister. I said my Niggras are in good shape. If you knew Mr. King, you know he treated his slaves right well."

Isaac grunted, shifted his eyes from Rufus and plopped back into his chair. Silent for a moment, he finally said, "What's your price?"

Rufus believed that he had convinced the buyer of the worthiness of his merchandise and answered brashly: "Why, the Natchez Daily Courier advertises a healthy slave at four hundred dollars. I'll let 'em go for less than that if you take the whole lot. Say thirty-thousand... three hundred each."

Two brawny Negro men had entered the room and stood behind Rufus. He felt their presence and recalled stories he had heard about Isaac Bankston. He was known to have whipped, or even killed a man whose point of view he disagreed with. Men who crossed Isaac Bankston were sometimes never seen again. A chill went up Rufus' spine and he dropped all pretenses.

"Give me two-fifty a head. You'll double your money," Rufus stammered.

"Ten thousand... a hundred dollars per. I don't negotiate."

Rufus impulsively stood ramrod tall, eyeing Isaac Bankston, silently wondering if he should defy him one more time. "Ah, but Mister Bankston, these is prime Niggras, good workers... well mannered. A hundred dollars each just ain't right." He turned slightly, glanced at the two bodyguards and rephrased his comments. "I mean, Suh, you are known throughout the territory as a fair-minded man. These slaves are insured... seen a doctor when they needed it."

"Means little to me."

"I'll drop my price a bit more. Give me two hundred a head or I'll take 'em to New Orleans."

Isaac Bankston bolted upright. "You'll take a hundred per or you'll take nothing. You stole these slaves. You whipped 'em and raped 'em, and you flat out mistreated them on the way up here. If it weren't for that Negro-loving' Quaker, Simon Rhoades, they'd have starved to death. My boys been watching you ever since you made your deal with that Woodville crowd."

Rufus now understood that he was in the company of a man much more sophisticated about business than he was. Obviously, Isaac Bankston had bested him. "I didn't harm 'em none."

Isaac Bankston had Rufus where he wanted him. He continued berating the overseer. "Ain't no slaving going on around these parts without me knowing about it. Hell, they're dying right out in front of my place. In a couple hours, they won't be worth a pine tree shilling. I'll be lucky to salvage half of them. It'll cost me plenty just to feed 'em... get 'em back in shape."

"You drive a hard bargain, Suh. I'll take cash—"

"Not so quick, Mr. Bohlinger." Isaac Bankston stepped from around the desk, nodding to his bodyguards.

He grabbed his hat from a hook by the door, slapped it on his leg and said, "Let's look 'em over... count what's left."

Rufus had to step quickly to keep up with the agile Isaac Bankston; he was a man of business. He told Rufus to wait alongside the road as he and his two aides trooped the line of exhausted captives. He stopped at several groups and spoke with them, Madison and Rebecca included. Returning to Rufus, he stood square in front of him, his fat jowls pulsating in and out. "Five thousand dollars. Take it and get off my place. Get out of Mississippi if you don't want to hang."

"Hell's fire, Sir. That's less than fifty—"

"You're a fool, Bohlinger. These people are Freemen." Isaac Bankston turned and pointed toward Madison. "That boy over there showed me his and his momma's papers."

Bankston clutched Madison's and Rebecca's certificates in his left hand, shaking them in Rufus's face. "You might as well have raided some farmer's barns, stole their branded cattle and tried to pass them off on me. I'll have to collect all these documents... make new papers and transfer the property over to me."

"Sheriff John Martin... Woodville... he approved it. He's waiting on his share. It's all legal—"

"... legal my grandpappy's ass. The laws of the state of Mississippi are right firm on buying and selling slaves. Are you familiar with the Louisiana Guarantee?"

"I know of the law."

"They're strict buyer-protection laws about slaving. Why, I could lose my whole business over this. Freed men is freed men."

"I didn't break no law, Mr. Bankston. I earned the right after ten years under Charles King. These slaves are properly mine."

Bankston gestured toward his two bodyguards. "These boys of mine... I cut 'em loose long ago. They're free, too. They stay with me because I treat 'em good. If somebody put 'em back in chains, I'd hunt the thief down and kill him, and then the man that had bought them. Might be a posse come up from Woodville an hour after you leave, looking to do the same to me. Five thousand or nothing."

"That's all?"

"They won't make it to New Orleans, either. You'll be digging graves all along the road. Take the five and git."

Rufus reached for Madison's and Rebecca's certificates of freedom and lit a match to them. "We'll pick up the rest."

Chapter Eleven

Oppression Renewed

Madison, Rebecca and all the other slaves were inside the cantonment by late afternoon, occupying small sheds where bedding, clean clothes, and cooking utensils had been provided. Young boys, uniformed in velvet pantaloons and baggy white shirts, brought in salted fish, pork, chicken, flour, fruits and vegetables. The boys looked plump and healthy and were utterly polite in their demeanor. They removed their furry round hats as they entered.

"Be water for washin' in the tubs out back," a lad of about fourteen told Rebecca. "This here grub be from Massa' Bankston. Says if ya'all need sumpin', I is ta' fetch it." He handed Rebecca a small crock of cooking oil, squeezed from corn. It was a luxury she had not seen since she and her grandmother had schucked corn in McCargoe's sheds.

"My' name is Jacob... Ah be a waitin' outside."

Rebecca smiled and thanked Jacob. She sat at a wooden table and laid her head in her arms. After a few hours rest and a bit to eat, she began to recovery from her ordeal. There was little sound from the other buildings, all of the slaves recuperating as best they could.

Rebecca finally stirred and asked Madison to help her start a fire in the hearth. Three other families had arrived and would share the small dwelling with them. Survival was their foremost concern and Rebecca accepted the challenge. She decided to cook a meal, wash and tend to the children, and restore order to their lives as well as she could.

Miss Mattie Henry, a chubby mother of six, gave orders to the children. "Get washed, pick off the nits... watch them brown ones; they has some real nasty bites. Now git!"

The Henry children knew instinctively that conditions had changed for the worse. They obeyed without question. Usually rowdy and fun provoking, they went in search of the wash troughs, while grave thoughts troubled their innocent hearts.

"Put on these new outfits, ya'all get back," Mattie shouted after them. "Ya'all look like pretty little glory angels."

Marcus Henry brought in an arm load of wood and prepared the fire. "I been a slave all my life... I ain't never seen so many provisions. Boys from the Wright clan... Ruby and her bunch... they killing' a hog... say it be for everybody."

Madison sat quietly, reciting prayers and asking for God's merciful intervention into their lives. He was confused and unsure of what was happening. Although indentured, he had never been treated as a slave. This was his first experience at subjugation. The others were adapting quickly, but his stomach churned with the deep hatred he held for Rufus Bohlinger, and it would not go away.

Marcus Henry found an old newspaper lying on a shelf. He crumpled several pages to light the fire. He couldn't read and considered newsprint useless except for "wiping asses and fire starter." Madison stopped him.

"Mr. Henry, don't burn that paper," Madison said. "Let me see it."

"I'll save you a page, Son... fire come first."

Madison took the page and examined it. In his melancholy state of mind, it was just something to do, something to settle his nerves. The others watched in awe of him, always amazed that one of their own could read. After glancing at the headlines, which were about politics and held no interest for him, he noticed the advertisement in the lower left hand corner:

Slaves! Slaves! Slaves!

Forks of the Road, Natchez.

"The Subscribers have just arrived in Natchez, and they are now stopping at Mr. Bankston's house, Forks of The Road, with a choice selection of slaves, consisting of mechanics, field hands, cooks, washers and ironers, and general house servants.

"They will be constantly receiving additions to the present supply during the season and will be sold at reasonable rates as can be afforded in this market. To those purchasers desiring it, the Louisiana Guarantee will be provided. Planters and others desirous of purchasing, are requested to call and see the slaves before purchasing elsewhere."

Madison handed the page back to Marcus who looked at it briefly, crumpled it into a tight ball, and then threw it into the fire.

"What did it say?" Mattie Henry asked.

"Nothing that will help us, Miss Mattie. It's about slaving here at the Forks. We are trapped... You can imagine what's going to happen to us." Madison was upset that the others, even his mother, made comments regarding the kindness of strangers and marveled over the abundance and quality of the foodstuffs they had been given. To him, they were adjusting too easily to their present circumstances and freedom was becoming too much a distant memory.

Jerimiah and Sappho Kelly, along with their three girls, swept up and arranged beds and bedding. Fifteen people would occupy their small quarters that night. Co-operation was imperative to their survival, and as slave families had always done under these conditions, they were exceptionally patient with one another.

Rebecca looked for onions and other spices to enhance her stew. Finding none, she asked if the Kelly children would venture beyond the shacks and find some wild onions. "Look for greens... poke salad, too," she said.

They raced out the door as soon as Rebecca suggested it, bumping into each other, laughing and falling as they squeezed through the doorway.

"Supper won't be ready 'till ya'all get back here. Don't get in a fuss with nobody," Sappho called after them.

The Kelly children; Nakira, sixteen years old; Gesenda, fourteen; and Genesia, twelve; had all miraculously recovered from their ordeal. They meandered casually between the evenly spaced rows of sheds, seeing others from the King plantation doing much the same as their own families. Children were naked, splashing each other in the huge washtubs. Cooking fires emitted the sweet aromas of yams, chicken, and beef roasts. No overseers or men on horseback were among them. Gradually they began to feel safe, slipping back into a frame of mind that all would be well, much as it had been at Kingland.

The Kelly children emerged from the last row of buildings and came upon a series of box cages, constructed of stout bamboo poles and elevated on short platforms about three feet off the ground. Row upon row, perhaps fifty cages in all, dotted the landscape. Broadleaf shade trees and tropical palm branches embraced the cage village, making it hardly visible without coming directly upon it. The children stopped dead in their tracks. Nakira clasped a bundle of onions to her breast and Gesenda dropped her collection of greens on the ground.

"Look at that," Genesia said. "We needs to tell momma." They turned and ran back to the cabin.

"Daddy! Momma!" They flew through the open door, out of breath, panting hard and screeching to a halt in front of their parents.

Nakira spoke first. Despite her youth, she was very much a woman, forced into maturity long before her time. "Daddy, we seen a bunch a Colored folk, all dressed in these same clothes and locked up in cages. They were just sitting, and white men were walking up and down lookin' in the cages—"

"Whoa, girl. Slow down. What did you see? Cages, you say?"

Gesenda interrupted. "They took one man out the cage and checked his teeth like you do a horse. We was scared."

"Then what happened...? What else did you see?" Jerimiah asked.

"Just men in them cages?" Marcus Henry wanted to know. "Any women?"

Genesia started to cry. "There was some women-folk... they took them into a big log house by the cages."

Jerimiah spoke softly, calming his children and then turned to Marcus. "Let's slip down there and see what's going on. I ain't gonna' let nothin' happen to our women and children."

Marcus nodded. "Let's go. You look after everybody, Madison... if we don't get back right quick."

Jerimiah and Marcus took a route different from that of the children. Using the tall grass and scrub brush that abounded in this secluded part of the camp, they were able to watch the slave inspections just as the children had described. Obscured by approaching evening shadows, they crept closer to the building that housed the women. Jerimiah peered through the window first, and then bent low to explain what he saw. "Marcus... look here... you ain't gonna' believe it."

Together, Marcus and Jerimiah peeked through the dirty glass panes. A scene of utter debauchery and evil unfolded before them: Naked, four young girls, molded with the near perfect bodies of youth, stood before several white buyers. The youngest girl, shivering with fear, looked to be perhaps twelve or thirteen-years old. The others were not much older. All of them exhibited slight European features with thin lips and slightly tapered noses. Two handsome male teenagers, rippling with the muscles of full-grown men, stood slightly aside from the girls.

"Turn right... slow. Halt! Now turn left... steady," Isaac Bankston commanded. With his riding crop, he prodded each youngster in the ribs, on the buttocks, and at the shoulder blades, requiring them to turn and display their naked human form. Embarrassed and crying, the girls tried to cover their most private parts with their hands. Isaac

smacked one child hard on the buttocks. "Get your hands
by your side. Turn around... Let's see your backside."

Having profiled the innocents to his satisfaction,
Bankston invited the buyers to have a closer look. He
patted his plump stomach. "Help yourselves, gentlemen.
I told you I housed the very best mixed breeds. They'll
make fine concubines... if you can afford them."

Laughter rose from the buyers. One tall man
raised the chin of the youngest girl with the handle of his
riding crop, looking into her dark eyes. Her tears did not
dissuade him. He walked behind her, separating the flesh
of her posterior and probing with his crop. He moved
slowly around her several times, finally stopping and staring at her lovely face. He reached and ran both hands up
and down her body, pausing to fondle her small breasts,
squeeze her slim waist, and then her thighs. Probing again
with his crop, he finally turned to Isaac and announced.
"I must try her. If she is all that she appears to be, I might
offer a thousand dollars."

"By all means, Sir." Isaac said. "Take whatever
liberties you desire. Use one of the rooms behind me.
Before you do, know that she goes out at no less than
three thousand."

"You must be mad," the tall man said. "Two
thousand dollars, perhaps... my top offer."

"Sold!" Isaac roared. "Take her and enjoy. You'll
make five times the price at retail in New Orleans."

The other youngsters were likewise inspected
and humiliated. One girl was rejected by a chubby middle-
aged buyer as being "too damn dark for the taste of my
clientele." She was taken back to the cages, while the others
were escorted into rooms and sexually ravaged by their
buyers—determining if they were fully qualified to serve

as concubines or prostitutes for the wealthy merchants and tourists of New Orleans.

The male slaves were inspected next. One buyer shook the shoulders of a lad, as if he were checking for loose bones. He inspected his back, the smoothness of his skin, and his anus. He stepped around to the front, squeezed his biceps, and then laid the youth's penis in his hand, fondling it for a moment. "This Negro has damn sure got a big organ. Circumcise him before I leave and I'll meet your price."

A dog barked nearby, causing Marcus and Jerimiah to come away from the window. Stooping low and sometimes crawling, they made their way back to their quarters. "Sappho don't never need to know about this" Jerimiah whispered. "God have mercy on those children and the souls of those wicked men."

"Pray all you want, brother," Marcus sneered. "There ain't no forgiveness for what we seen. Those men are going straight to hell."

Marcus and Jerimiah entered their cabin, revealing little of what they had witnessed. They did not wish to frighten the children or the women any further. Madison listened to their scant description of the cages, but sensed that they had more to tell.

Madison stood. He now towered over his mother, standing more than six feet. "You all know what's going on. We're to be fattened up... separated. One by one, we'll be put in those cages for sale."

Madison slammed his fist onto a table demanding the attention of everyone in the room. "We are free people! They can't do this to us. Are you all willing to go back into slavery? I am not. Mr. Bankston has our papers and must let us go. There are laws—"

Marcus Henry appraised Madison. "You might not know it, Son, but we're already back in slavery. Do you think Massa' Bankston is gonna' give up them papers... cut us loose? I'm thinking that Ruth and Charles King ruined your good sense with all that book learnin'."

Rebecca turned from her task of preparing sleeping places for the children. She clutched a thin blanket to her breast and looked longingly at her son. She felt deep regret that she had shielded Madison from the realities of slavery. She knew in her heart that they were bound for another plantation, separation, and a lifetime of toil and abuse. The good days had passed.

"The Lord does hear our prayers, Madison, but sometimes he has other plans for us," Rebecca said. "You can be sure He's moving things around, but His answer will come in a way you won't expect. Keep on praying... never lose hope."

Marcus Henry decided to diffuse the tension. "Children, don't ya'all worry none 'bout them cages. We gonna' eat real good tonight... sleep like your snoring old daddy do. We'll say our prayers and then see what the morning gonna' bring us."

"Lord spare us from another plantation..." Mattie Henry wailed.

"Going to a plan'ashun' might be a blessing', Mattie," Marcus said. "There is worse things might could happen to us...to the girls"

The supper was delicious; filling and nutritious. The conversation centered on their unknown future and they were optimistic, speculating that the Lord would deliver them into the hands of a kind master.

"Maybe we'll be sold to good people like Mr. King and Ruth," Rebecca said in an almost jovial voice.

Madison rose from the table, his meal barely touched. "What's wrong with all of you? You give up so easily. We are not slaves!"

"So we ain't slaves... well then, what are we?" Jerimiah asked.

"Miss Ruth set us loose! Rufus Bohlinger didn't have any right.... I'll see Mr. Bankston... tell him straight away that we are going back to the King place. Then my mother and I are leaving!"

Silence settled over the group. The men hung their heads and the children stared at Madison. By their stillness, he assumed that they were too timid; too long a slave to contemplate rebellion.

"How can you accept this? One man did this to us: Rufus Bohlinger. He is not God. I'm not going into those cages and neither is my mother."

Mattie broke the spell with a call for prayers. The evening finished with everyone retiring early. They were still very much exhausted from their agonizing journey, and after the food, sleep came upon them quickly. The elders slept in the three wooden beds while the children snuggled up side by side on the floor. Madison slept on a bench.

Chapter Twelve

Lost Hope

The crowing of a rooster and the braying of a mule brought them up just before dawn. Rebecca asked that the fire be lit: she had cooking to do.

Madison rubbed the sleep from his eyes and surveyed the room. *How can she put up with this? How is it she goes on as if we were never free, as if we are destined to be slaves*? A fire burned in his belly and the seeds of an escape plan began to form in his mind. Somehow, he would be free again.

Marcus Henry and Jerimiah Kelly took the children outside to the toilet—a wooden outhouse—and to fetch fresh water. At the well, they heard a rider approaching. In the early light, they recognized Isaac Bankston coming toward them. He rode a black stallion; a long-barrel musket lay across the saddle. Two black men rode behind him. Both had whips in their hands.

"Morning, ya'all." Isaac Bankston said. "I take it your bellies are full of good victuals and you been well-rested? Ya'all doing all right?" He smiled.

The children gathered close behind their parents.

Marcus Henry spoke first. "Yes, Massa'... we been getting along fine. Thank ya', Massa'."

"Um hum, that's right, Suh," Jerimiah Kelly said. "The children and womenfolk all feeling better after that long walk up from the King place." Jerimiah was sparked by something Madison had said. "What's to happen to us? We are free men.... Mrs. King gave us papers."

Isaac Bankston steadied his horse as it agitated for movement. "Freemen? Papers? I don't know about no free men and no papers. I bought the lot of ya' fair and square. You'll live well here in the cabins for a while. There's plenty of food, nobody will bother you. Obey my rules. Don't wander off or I'll come get ya'."

"Yes, Massa'," Marcus said.

"Come the middle of the month, buyers coming in from Alabama and Georgia. You'll have new homes, new masters. You men need to get a little meat on those bones."

"Yes, Suh'," Jerimiah said.

Marcus and Jerimiah knew exactly where they stood. Their feigned humility had satisfied Isaac Bankston. Jerimiah approached the slave trader's horse. "Beg yo' pardon, Massa'. Any wagons going by the King place?"

"Why?"

Jerimiah grew bolder. "Suh, we had to leave most of our things... we want to send a message to Mrs. King."

Isaac Bankston chewed on a large wad of tobacco. He pondered for a moment. "Maybe you ain't heard, Boy. The King place burned down last night."

"Oh my," Jerimiah said. He threw a hand across his mouth.

Marcus Henry stepped closer to Isaac Bankston. "And Miss Ruth?"

"She burned up with it. You are my Negroes now

and don't you forget it. That damn Charles King ruined ya'all. Get that freedom foolishness out of your heads and get back to your women." Isaac Bankston spit brown juice at their feet, turned his horse and rode off.

Marcus, Jerimiah, and the children walked slowly back to their cabin, their shoulders slumped and their heads hung low. Marcus picked up his youngest and carried him in his arms.

Isaac Bankston rode throughout the cabins, the outhouses, and the watering holes carrying on much the same conversation he had with Marcus and Jerimiah. By the time he finished his morning rounds, the former free men and women of Charles and Ruth King knew without a doubt that they were under the rule of a merciless oppressor. They would never be free again.

Madison whiled away the next several days helping his mother and the others make life bearable. On one occasion, Isaac Bankston stopped by and checked his teeth, biceps, joints, and then made him drop his shirt so that he could inspect his back. "Just one mark.... Good. Never been fully whipped, eh, Boy?"

Isaac stepped back, satisfaction glowing in his eyes over Madison's physique, and pleased with himself over the clever deal he had foisted on Rufus Bohlinger. "You're a fine specimen of a man, Washington. I hear you can read... handle horses.

"Some."

Isaac smacked Madison on the thigh with his crop. "Some what?" You speak to me proper, Boy."

"Yes, Massa'."

"Might be a while 'afore a buyer comes by... pays what you're worth. Now, change your clothes so that folks will know you're available." He threw Madison a bundle of clothing.

All of the newly arrived slaves were required to wear the corduroy uniforms with white cotton shirt and black fur cap, and they hated it. It was a mark of servitude, a clear sign of being beholding to the master. They were men and women without souls they could call their own and the uniforms advertised it.

"You leave my outfit behind when you get sold. Don't forget it," Isaac said.

When the slaves appeared healthy, had gained weight and any evidence of disease or ailments were obliterated, they were taken to the sale cages. As their hour of departure and the inevitable separation from their spouses and children approached, Isaac Bankston kept them shackled and guarded. He and his partner, John Armstead, did not usually auction slaves. Instead, they announced the price, and that was that. They seldom bargained except to offer a child or an elderly person as an added incentive to move a healthy slave.

Madison and Rebecca grew accustomed to the pace in the forward cabins. They had yet to see the cages. They, as well as the others who had arrived with them, were regaining their strength from the ample foods and idle time. Isaac Bankston did not require that they work except to till the garden and perform normal household chores.

Two weeks passed, and then one by one, fathers and mothers, brothers and sisters, were separated from their families and taken to the cages. There were no tearful good-byes, no prolonged hugs. Isaac came in the middle of the night, at dawn, and all throughout the day, selecting candidates for sale. Trades and transactions went on at all hours when visitors arrived. Isaac was eager for cash flow and he didn't like to hold his buyers up for very long.

Isaac brought slave after slave onto a platform to be viewed and inspected by the buyers. He described their physical features and verified their skills and history of craftsmanship. Finally announcing the price, he stepped aside for the buyers to inspect the merchandise. If an offer to buy did not occur within a few minutes, Isaac handed the neck chain to one of his black bodyguards and the slave was returned to his cage.

Buyers who agreed with Isaac's demands paid in cash or bank certificates. One of the black lackeys provided bills of sale and courthouse registration papers. In an hour, they were off the property and headed throughout Louisiana, Mississippi, Alabama, Georgia, and other slave holding states. Between their operations in Virginia and the Forks of the Road at Natchez, Isaac Bankston and John Armstead set and controlled the prices of slaves in the south. Other slavers tried to mimic them, but few could compare with the human traffic they generated. Their perceptive business sense and customer service attributes had allowed them to process almost one-hundred thousand slaves during the twenty-years they had been in business.

On a cool September morning, Rebecca rose to start the fire. Without notice, Isaac Bankston burst through the door and called for Marcus Henry. Mattie and the children were barely awake as Isaac and the two guards dragged Marcus out the door. He shouted his love for her and the children over commands to "shut up" and the manhandling he received. That afternoon it was Jerimiah Kelly's turn, then Sappho's. Over the next few days, Mattie, her children, and then the Kelly children were taken away. Although they were caged in close proximity to one another, they were forbidden to speak or call out. Armed guards patrolled every few feet. There was no disobedience, few words, and little hope for escape.

The men were isolated from the women and children, and they were the first to go. Marcus Henry was sold to a Kansas wheat farmer who had traveled far and paid top dollar. Mid-West farmers usually came to barter grain, buy building materials, and purchase a slave or two while they were visiting. Isaac was forced to offer a teen-age girl, pregnant with her first child, as an incentive for consummating the deal. Marcus and the girl were loaded atop a wagon stacked with fat-pine boards. Marcus waved good-bye as the wagon lumbered down the road, but no one came out to see him.

Mattie was sold to a Methodist church group from Zachary, Louisiana and left the next day. She would serve as a cook and cleaning lady. She was allowed to take one of her children. The others, growing healthy and holding forth promise for a lifetime of hard work, were held for future bargaining.

Jerimiah, Sappho, Gesenda and Genesia Kelly were sold to an estate near Clinton, Louisiana, just north of Baton Rouge. It was a beginning town and needed plenty of slave labor to construct the new homes of politicians, wealthy lawyers, doctors, and other professionals who were moving there to be near the proposed, new State Capital. As a family, the Kelly's had been purchased at premium prices. They were fortunate to serve a decent master who neither abused nor neglected them. Nakira, the fairest and loveliest of the Kelly girls, was taken into the buyers lodge with a metal collar and chain around her neck. Her parents or siblings never saw her again.

Chapter Thirteen

The Breeding Pens

Several weeks passed and most of the families from the King plantation had been sold or traded away. Their destinations and uncertain futures were unknown to the others, their children, wives and relatives. Madison and Rebecca were unmolested, remaining in their cabin, helping others as the need arose. On an afternoon when trading had slowed to a trickle, Isaac Bankston walked through the door. Madison knew he was next to go to the cages and he mentally vowed to die before he'd be separated from his mother.

"Well, well... Miss Rebecca, they tell me you're a mighty fine cook."

"Yes, Massa'."

Isaac patted his stomach and laughed. "I've not had the pleasure of tasting your victuals, but folks tell me I should."

"Yes, Massa'. Thank You, Massa'."

Madison listened quietly, anger and frustration welling up in his chest. *White devils don't have kind words for slaves. What's his scheme...?*

Isaac continued: "Judging from the looks of those boys you been feeding, you damn sure have a skill for cookery. Why, that Henry boy bought six hundred dollars."

Rebecca and Madison remained outwardly passive, hiding their mutual disdain for Isaac Bankston.

"That other team—the Kelly's and the children—they went out at nineteen hundred. I appreciate you helping to get 'em ready."

Rebecca, now alarmed, shuddered at the thought that she was partly responsible for bringing her friends back to health and thereby readying them for sale. For a moment she regretted that she had done so. *I should have fed them small portions. But there was nothing I could do... he'd have sold them eventually.*

There was some redemption in knowing that high priced slaves went to the wealthiest owners and perhaps they would have better living conditions.

"You won't be sold just yet, Woman. You'll move up to the main house. I intend for you to be one of my permanents... cook for the others." Isaac reached and placed his hands on Rebecca's slim waist as if he were measuring her. He squeezed her slightly and stared at her breasts for a moment. "Um hum... please me... you won't be sold. Get your things."

Madison seethed inside, recognizing Isaac's thinly concealed lust for Rebecca. Although he had been shielded from the incidences of white masters and their teenage sons roaming the slave quarters after dark, he had heard stories of how they lusted after young black girls. Many a 'yellow' boy had been born in the houses of the King plantation.

Young men, the nearly adult children of the King overseers and other white employees, often barged into the slave quarters at night choosing whomever they desired for the lust game they played. At times they selected a young girl for sex, and sometimes they took a young boy. After using him up, forcing him to perform the most vile sex acts; they often castrated him with hunting knives, leaving the boy in the fields to either bleed to death or crawl back to his mother. Charles King forbade the practice, but left it to Rufus Bohlinger to enforce his rules.

On impulse, Isaac Bankston reached and fondled one of Rebecca's breasts. "You're a well-figured woman, Rebecca..."

Madison rose to defend his mother but she shot him a glance that stopped him in his tracks. "Why thank you, Massa'," she cooed. I'll be a good worker. And my boy here... Madison?"

"Yes, your boy.... I've been considering him. You can bring him along. I'll have later use for him." Isaac considered Madison for a moment, studying his large frame. "Pick out rooms in the main lodge, I'll be coming by from time to time." He slapped his crop against his thigh and left.

Madison's heart raced and he added another name to the list of men he intended to kill someday. "Momma, do you understand what that pig is saying to you? He intends to take you—"

Rebecca looked sheepishly at her son and hung her head low, her chin against her chest. "We have no choice, Bula Matadi. God knows what we must do to survive. He'll not hold me responsible. ...I pray."

Tears dotted her eyes and Madison nodded his understanding, then he took her in his arms. "I'm sorry, Momma, I'm so sorry."

By dusk they had moved into the large main

quarters near the front gate. It was made of logs, almost forty-feet long and thirty paces wide. It sat adjacent to the main office building, allowing Isaac and his bodyguards to watch the comings and goings of the occupants. The dwelling boasted ten rooms; the walls sculpted from coarse pinewood. Eight rooms were set aside as sleeping quarters. There was little else except a kitchen, a pantry and a large general-purpose room. A fireplace sat in the center and served as a cooking hearth as well as a means for heating the entire lodge. The floors were rough unfinished pine, but covered with several colorful carpets; obviously woven by slave hands. Although small and sparsely furnished, Rebecca and Madison chose adequate rooms next to each other.

Rebecca cleaned and made the place livable. Madison spent the first few days helping with chores, chopping firewood, carrying water and the dozens of other tasks it took run a household. Soon, six other slaves moved in. Three young girls and three boys stood at the open door, timid in their demeanor and asking Madison if they could enter.

"Massa' tell us come up in here... I am Joshua," one of the lads offered.

Madison had never seen them before but he welcomed them, ushering them inside. He introduced them to Rebecca, and then assisted each youngster to their rooms. By late evening, Rebecca had fed them and instructed them on her rules, assigning household chores to each. Madison led them in prayer, and then bluntly asked about their personal lives. "Where ya'all come from?" he inquired. "How did you end up here... what did Isaac Bankston tell you?"

Caroline Andrews and Elizabeth Cullen were half-sisters. Milinda Joiner was an orphan of unknown background. She had taken her previous plantation owner's last name as she had been instructed to do. The teenage boys: Joshua, Matthew, and Caleb, were brought to the Forks only a few days before. Their stories were typical of slaves: They had each been bought and sold several times over at slave markets ranging from South Carolina to New Orleans. None of them knew their parents, had any idea of their African legacies, and had been worked or beaten into submission long before they reached adolescence.

Several days passed and Madison observed that all of them were hard working, seemingly happy, and went about their few duties with smiles on their faces. The sometimes broke into song, or danced as the others clapped hands and sang. They became friends rather quickly, and Madison, by virtue of his age, articulation and physical stature, became the natural leader of the group. They looked to him for advice.

"Why Massa' put us up in here?" Joshua asked. "I just wanna' know what I supposed to do... stay outta' trouble."

The others asked much the same questions but Madison had no answers. "We'll find out real soon, I'm sure."

The first week in their new quarters passed without incident. After completing their chores, they ventured out in the late afternoons to play games of stickball or simply to investigate the property. Isaac Bankston walked by a few times and said nothing, so they assumed their excursions were not offensive to him.

Milinda was attracted to Madison, finding opportunities to press against him during their ball playing. When he shunned her advances, she fell to teasing him. "Can't catch me!" Milinda taunted, after throwing a pail of water on Madison's back. She took off running between the houses and through the garden.

Madison gave chase, feigning anger at the dousing. Beyond the patches of beans and small vegetables, they raced into a cornfield where Madison grabbed her waist and together they stumbled onto the soft earth. She panted for a moment, her firm breasts heaving, and then looked up at him as he lay atop her.

"Kiss me, damn you," she said.

Madison was speechless. His loins were on fire and his heart raced. He opened his dry mouth and pressed his lips against hers. Her tongue entered his mouth and he did the same, probing her moist oral cavity. She was hot inside and he felt her thrusting pelvis push hard against him. Together they reached for his manhood, delirious for the impending pleasure.

"Hey, where are ya'all?" Caroline shouted as she and the others thrashed their way through the foliage. "You can't hide.... We are coming to get you."

Startled, Madison and Milinda jumped to their feet, brushing off dirt and straightening their clothes. Milinda regained her composure quickly, but Madison's sheepish grin revealed all. "Damn, damn, and double damn," Milinda said.

Elizabeth and Joshua poked their heads through the cornrows, followed by the others. Madison and Milinda acted as if the incident was entirely innocent, but Elizabeth teased. "I know what ya'all was fixin' to do. Massa' gonna' whup ya' both good and put ya' in a cage."

"We weren't doing anything," Madison said firmly. He reached for Milinda's hand but found a cornstalk instead.

"I'm scared, let's get out of here afore Massa'

catches us," Matthew said. He was the most frail of the boys and timorous by nature.

The ever-present danger of a whipping by the white slave master motivated them to move quickly out of the field and into the sunlight. They headed back to the main house, Madison holding Milinda's hand as she skipped along. From his office window, Isaac Bankston smiled. "Our breeders are starting to find each other," John. I told you I'd have new sources for slaves when you got back from Virginia. Might take a few years but we're going to be here a long, long time."

John Armstead laughed. "Leave it to you, Isaac, and I won't have to travel to Richmond much longer. We'll raise our own. Too damn bad they ain't rabbits."

Isaac turned from the window and looked at his longtime business partner. "Guess it's time I put them to work. The ignorant fools are just now getting to know each other. See that big buck, Washington... looks like he found him a mate but the others are too slow or too damn stupid to do what should come natural."

That evening Isaac came to their lodge and told Rebecca to gather the youngsters. He moved about the main room, pairing up each boy and girl. "You, Caroline... stand over there with Caleb." He examined the couple and remarked: "You'll make a healthy child soon enough. Understand?"

Rebecca gasped as Isaac Bankston continued his arrangements. Repulsed, she suddenly realized what he intended for the youngsters and why they had been afforded such unusual lodgment and fair treatment. The children were to propagate offspring; more slaves for the master.

Isaac Bankston finished pairing off the couples. Without shame or hesitation, he spoke bluntly. His ever-present riding crop beat steadily against his palm. "Starting tonight, you girls and boys are going to sleep with each other. You'll perform the connubial acts that are so natural to your race. I expect you to be with child real soon. If not, you are useless to me and you'll be sold off. Any questions?"

Matthew began to weep quietly and Rebecca held his hand. Madison and the others needed no further explanations

"Washington, you take the Joiner girl. You boys share the other two girls as your needs arise. Now, get busy," Isaac turned and stomped out of the lodge, slamming the door as he went.

Madison and Milinda did not obey Isaac's order immediately. He lay alone for several nights listening to the sounds of passion emanating from the other rooms. At first, the episodes lasted only a few minutes, but eventually, the unmistakable cries of long and passionate lovemaking echoed throughout the lodge. By the end of the second week, numerous sexual liaisons erupted all during the night. Madison felt ashamed and wondered if God would throw them all into a fire on Judgment Day.

Near midnight on the first Monday of a new month, Madison awakened to voices and movement from Rebecca's room. He heard Isaac's loud cough then the sound of boots hitting the floor. Intuitively knowing that his mother was serving at the pleasure of the master, he knelt and prayed for her—for all of them.

In the morning, Rebecca was somewhat flustered as she spoke to Madison, but she said nothing of the goings-on in her room. The days became weeks and Isaac visited Rebecca's room regularly. After a night of forced love making, she'd assume a mask of absolute composure the following day. Nothing was ever said about it.

During a particularly busy night, Madison heard the unmistakable squealing of Caroline, deep in the throes of passion. In another room, Elizabeth moaned and Caleb shouted. Later, Madison heard the voices of Matthew and Joshua arguing over who they would service next. On one occasion, the voices of older men, white men, echoed behind the walls. It was driving Madison crazy.

Not a sound emitted from Milinda's room and Madison swore that he'd protect her with his life if he did hear anything. On one rare, quiet evening, after midnight, a soft tapping fell on Madison's ears. He rose from his bed, wrapped a cloth around his naked body and opened the door for Milinda. He reached and pulled her tender body toward him. Between their hot kisses, Madison asked, "What took you so long?"

They fell to his bed where Madison nestled his head between her ample breasts, kissing them, rubbing the nipples as she begged him to do. He began licking her body, up and down, between her breasts and her lower belly. Milinda held his head, pulling him to her lips. She kissed him fiercely, describing the things she wanted him to do to her and he complied. Drenched in sweat and his body on fire, he directed his manhood into the soft wet cleft between her legs. In moments, the two souls became one, floating on clouds of sexual fulfillment.

Madison instantly became the lover, the lifelong protector of Milinda Joiner. In a month, they married near the cornfield with Matthew and Caleb holding the broomstick. Joshua served as best man; Caroline and Elizabeth, witnesses and bridesmaids. Rebecca officiated, joining them in matrimony and issuing her blessings. She cooked a superb meal that night as a means of celebration. After cleaning up, she returned to her room and the noises commenced after midnight, as usual.

Madison and Milinda no longer maintained separate rooms, but slept together as man and wife. Within weeks she was pregnant and in the winter of 1840, when Madison was twenty-one and Milinda was about eighteen, she gave birth to a healthy baby boy. They named him Isaac, after Madison's father. Isaac Bankston beamed at the news.

"Did you hear that?" he asked John Armstead. "They named that boy after me. They should all be carrying children soon. If this all works out like I expect it will, I'll put twenty of them to breeding."

Armstead, a tall wiry man, raised his head from his accounting ledgers and stood. He scratched his head with a bony finger, and then smiled at his partner. "You might be selling your own son, you don't stop with that Rebecca. She looks to be getting a little plump around the middle." He laughed and said, "Hell, I know you pretty good, Isaac. You would indeed sell him."

"Damn right... but that won't happen. I'd terminate it if it were true.

"How would you do that... shoot her?"

"No. My God, man.... Nothing like that. You sure she's getting plump? I hadn't took notice."

Chapter Fourteen

Death At The Lodge

In mid-February 1841, Madison and Milinda awakened to unusually loud sounds coming from Rebecca's room. Young Isaac nestled between them. Rebecca screamed horribly, once, and then was apparently muffled. Madison shot out of bed and took the three steps to his mother's room, kicking open the door. An unknown man, a thin middle-aged white male, leaned over Rebecca with a pillow in his hands. He paid no attention to Madison or the other youngsters who had heard the cry and came running.

"What are you doing?" Madison shouted. He rushed to the bed, sat on the edge and took Rebecca's limp body in his arms. He rocked her for a moment, observing a wide gash on her forehead; the blood matting her hair and running into her right eye. Her head flopped back and forth at the neck and she was not breathing.

"Momma! Momma! What happened? Wake up! Speak to me!" Madison wailed. Moaning and shouting his petitions over and over, he soon laid Rebecca aside. Her body was still, growing cold beneath his touch. Madison knew that there was nothing he could do for her. She was dead. He gently laid her head on the bed, and then lunged for the assailant, grabbing him by the throat and shouting, "Murderer... you killed my mother! Damn you!"

Isaac Bankston, John Armstead, and other men burst into the room. Isaac drew his pistol. "Get your Niggra hands off of him, Boy... or you'll end up like her. Now everybody settle down. What's going on here?"

John Armstead's bodyguards grabbed Madison's arms and pulled them from the stranger's throat. He sucked air and rubbed his neck, his eyes as big as saucers.

"He beat her... then he smothered her!" Madison screamed. "I'll kill him!" He lunged for the man again, but the others restrained him.

"You must explain yourself, Mr. Walkup," Isaac Bankston demanded. "I invite my Kentucky buyer for a little fun and you kill my prize whore?"

Mr. Walkup, recovering his composure, replied, "That's not it at all, Sir. I didn't kill her. I suspect she was startled... seeing me at this late hour. She became hysterical. I should have knocked... spoken out at first, but I didn't. I reached out to calm her, but she collapsed and struck her head on the footboard. I believe her heart arrested—"

"Liar," Madison bellowed. "Why the pillow?"

"I was simply placing it under her head... trying to comfort her. I didn't kill her."

"Well, it sounds rather peculiar to me, too, Mr. Walkup, but I'll take your word for it," Isaac said. "We done business 'afore.... Pay me half price for the dead slave and we'll call it even. No harm done."

Enraged that there would be no justice for his mother, Madison lunged, throwing off the restraining hands with one shrug. He slammed Mr. Walkup to the floor with a massive blow, and then fell on top of him, strangling him once again. "You murdering, lying son of Satan—"

Isaac Bankston fired his pistol across Madison's head then shoved the hot barrel against his temple. "Let him go or I'll scatter your brains all over this room. Now!" He pulled the hammer back and took up the slack in the trigger.

Milinda, crying and wailing, wrapped her arms around Madison's shoulders. "Please, please, Madison, let him go. He'll kill you!"

The only voice Madison could hear through his rage had made its point. He released his hold on his mother's murderer and stood. Suddenly, an uncontrollable rage took hold of him. With a quick flick of his hand, Madison disarmed Isaac Bankston and grabbed him by the throat, squeezing ever harder and harder as the slave trader slumped to the floor. His neck snapped and in a few moments, he was dead. Madison held his grip on Isaac's neck until a pistol smashed across his head, rendering him unconscious.

Violent hands dragged him outside and across the yard. Under the light of amber torches, several men manacled him at the wrists, and then lashed him to a ring at the top of a stout oaken pole.

Barely conscious, Madison heard John Armstead shout, "Throw some water on that murderin' Niggra! I want him to feel every bit of the thrashing I'm going to lay on him."

The two bodyguards complied and doused Madison with several buckets of water.

"I'll take your lash," John Armstead said, snatching a long bullwhip from a guard. "I want the pleasure of killing him myself. If he ain't dead when I'm finished, I'll hang him when the sun rises."

Madison was not quite conscious when the first blow fell across his back and right shoulder, cutting deep into his flesh. The sting brought him fully alert as adrenaline pumped through his veins. "Jesus... have mercy!" he cried out.

The second and third blows fell equally as hard and blood oozed from his wounds. Madison's breath came in short gasps. He nearly fainted as the fourth and fifth strokes fell. A crowd had formed, bringing lanterns with them to light the sky and watch a man being beaten to death.

"Kill 'em... kill 'em," a puny white man shouted from the ranks. "Whup 'em good!"

Other whites joined the chorus, screaming for Madison's blood and then a hanging. Caroline and Elizabeth held Milinda back as she bawled and wailed for her lover. Joshua, Matthew and Caleb fidgeted, standing silently, watching the merciless spectacle. The beating continued and Madison cried out the names of prophets, as if they would somehow rescue him. "Elijah, please!" Madison yelled as blow ten fell. "Jacob...!"

At blow twenty Madison's back was a mass of minced and shredded flesh, lying beneath a sea of scarlet blood. He had fainted sometime after blow eighteen. He slumped, straining the shackles—no longer feeling any pain. His last conscious thought was of Rebecca.

John Armstead stopped suddenly. Sweat dripped from his brow and he struggled for air, panting rapidly. He coiled the whip and turned to the crowd. "You Niggras... you see what you have done! You see what will happen to you if you rile me!

"Can we cut him down now, Massa'?" Matthew timidly asked.

"Take him to a cage," John Armstead bellowed. He ain't good enough to die by the whip. He'll hang at first light." He strode toward his main office, red-faced, puffing air and swearing.

Madison collapsed in a heap when Matthew, Joshua and Caleb took him down. Milinda rushed forward and held his head in her lap, begging God to let him live. Her hands, covered with the blood of her husband, caressed him, matting his hair and streaking his face. She wept like a child, but soon composed herself and tried to comfort him with loving words. Before long she realized that her pity would do him little good and she released him to the guards. Without molesting him further, they helped him to one of the cages, threw him in and secured the door with a loop of thick hemp. They returned to Mr. Armstead and asked for instructions.

"I'm gonna' hang that bastard in the morning," Armstead said. "Killing' Isaac like he did... Someone get the sheriff over here so we can make it legal."

Madison lay semiconscious on a mat of moist and smelly straw. All the tragedy that had transpired over the past few hours raced through head, but his only thoughts were of his beautiful mother, Rebecca. In all her loveliness, she appeared as an apparition and he wanted to go to her, hold her, and protect her. No plan of action, no thought of escape entered his mind. He surrendered to the inevitable; he would die in the morning. Then he would be with his mother, forever.

Meanwhile, Milinda, Caroline, Elizabeth, Matthew, Caleb and Joshua put a rescue plan into motion. "Madison is not going to swing at the end of a rope," Milinda announced. "Let's get to work."

Elizabeth and Matthew searched the barns and

sheds, scooping up large spider webs by the light of their torch. In twenty minutes, they had a pouch full of the delicate, sticky lace.

"What we going to do with this, 'Lizabeth?" Matthew asked.

"Stop the bleeding, Matthew. "It's clean and it sucks up the blood. We need to paste it on his cuts right quick. An old slave woman told me the spider cobs has got something that makes the bleedin' stop and the healing start."

At Milinda's sudden direction, Caleb ran south toward the Rhoades plantation. At about four-thirty in the morning, he was banging on the door of Amos Jefferson, a black man known to have influence among the landowners, overseers, and slave merchants. Amos opened the door an inch, peering out into the darkness. "Who there? What you want in da' middle a da' night?"

"Trouble up at the Forks," Caleb whispered. "Been a killing. They gonna' hang Madison."

"A hanging? Well, come in and sit, Son," Amos said. He wrapped his arm around the teenager, drawing him into this cabin. "Now, who is dis' Madison fella'?"

Caroline crept through the alleys of the darkened slave city. She tapped lightly on the door of Martha Lightfoot, an elderly black woman who had lived at the Forks most of her life. She possessed extraordinary skills for fashioning carpets, quilts and making clothing. When her talents became known to Isaac Bankston, he utilized her as a seamstress, supplying uniforms and blankets to the slaves.

The door cracked open, exposing only a large black eye set high above a flat broad nose. "Go 'way. What do you want commin' here 'afore the rooster crow?"

"I'm sorry, Miss Martha. I'm Caroline... been a whuppin'. I need one of your blankets."

The door opened wider. Martha gazed at Caroline, assessing her features in the dim light. "Youse' one of them trollops from up the big house, ain't ya'? I heard the ruckus. Who been whupped?"

"Madison Washington. He killed Mr. Bankston... somebody killed Rebecca. They are going to hang him come daylight. We gotta' help him. Please let me have one of those escape quilts people talk about."

Martha weighed the possible consequences of her generosity if she complied with Caroline's request.

"Come in, ya' wide-eyed child. I has one... a pretty wrap... finished it just last night."

Caroline entered the smelly hut, squinting her eyes against the dim light of burning fireplace embers. Martha reached on top of a cupboard, retrieved and unfolded a brilliantly colored shawl, about four feet square. Martha beckoned to Caroline. "So, the big buck done killed Isaac, huh? Good... 'um glad of it. Come over by the fire and I show ya' what ya' needs to know."

Caroline accepted the shawl from Martha, and then held it to the light. The red, green, and black cotton strands wove an intricate pattern of small squares, triangles, and circles. It was a unique design, but more importantly, a clever blueprint for deception.

"Look close, Child. I show you the codes." Martha pointed a crooked finger at the bottom right corner of the piece. "Black shapes is black folk. When they beside a red square, it mean trouble. If'n they beside a green square, it be safe."

"Where we... where does he start from?"

"Here on the left." Martha pointed to a black

circle next to a red square. "This be the Forks." She moved a bony finger across shawl: "Down here be Amos Jeff'son. ...Rhoades plan'ashun'. He start from there."

Caroline suddenly became aware that she was looking at the secret escape codes of the Underground Railroad. She had heard about them, but most folks said they were a myth. On this shawl, the Rhoades plantation appeared as a black triangle within a green circle.

"Then what should he do?"

"Any green is safe. He goes right from there, then he goes up. Tell him to go north. When a pattern changes, it be another state along the road to freedom. Four states up and he be in Canadee." Martha folded the shawl and tucked it under Caroline's arm. "Take it and go. Good luck to him."

"Thank you Miss Martha. Madison will be taking that road to freedom now."

Martha smiled broadly, revealing two lonely yellow teeth. "I don't give the code ta' just anybody.... I kinda' cotton to the looks of that big stallion. I'll make you a blanket, too, Honey... if'n you want to go with him"

Caroline embraced the old woman, thanking her again, and then sped back to the lodge. Panting hard, she held the shawl up to Milinda and the others. "I got it!"

"Good girl," Milinda said. She looked up from the small cotton bag she was stuffing with survival items. She reached for the shawl, rolled it tightly, and then packed it into the bag.

Joshua sharpened a large butcher knife with a whetstone. "What's he gonna' do with this?"

Milinda was assembling strips of dried jerky and preparing a leather flask of water. "He's going to cut his way to freedom, Joshua. It's almost sunup... let's go."

Milinda and Joshua crept through the morning dew, inching their way toward the cages. In moments, they were kneeling behind Madison's cage. He had not moved for several hours. The roaming guards paid little attention to him. He was lifeless, lying there at the bottom of his pen. The guards rendezvoused at the end of the dwellings where they smoked and made small talk, speculating whether Mr. Walkup had actually murdered Rebecca or had accidentally spooked her into dying of fright.

"Bankston put him up to it," a young trustee said.

"Best hush yo' mouth.... Yo' be swingin' with him," another said. They fell to discussing whether they should attend the hanging of a brother slave, but concluded that the Massa' would insist upon it anyway.

"Madison... Madison, " Milinda called softly. She reached through the cage and felt the hair on his head. "Madison, wake up... wake up."

He stirred slightly, still somewhat incoherent from the beating. He had lost a large amount of blood and an excruciating thirst scorched his mouth. He raised his head an inch or two. "Milinda?"

Milinda and Joshua reached through the bars and applied the spider web to his back. Almost immediately, Madison's bleeding stopped and he sensed it. "Water, I need water," he begged.

Joshua slipped the water flask between the bars and laid it at Madison's cheek. "Drink, brother, drink."

Madison rose up on his elbows, sucking the cool liquid from the skin.

"Take this knife," Milinda said. "You gotta' move fast.... The escape codes are on the shawl. Go south to Woodville. Find the Rhoades place... find Amos Jefferson."

Chapter Fifteen

The Great Escape

Madison slipped into and out of consciousness, barely hearing the escape instructions. He gathered enough strength to roll onto his side and stare into the whispers. Again, he heard Milinda speak, softly calling his name. He whispered: "Rebecca? Is it you"

"It's Milinda... Milinda... Rebecca is gone, Madison... Madison, Honey... are you all right?"

Madison raised his head and groaned.

"Shh, don't say nothing. Just listen... I'm going to slip you a knife. Cut the rope that holds the door when you're ready. You have the codes... get away fast. Head to the Rhoades place."

Madison came alert at the sound of his lover's voice. He searched the cage and his surroundings. "Give me the knife."

Milinda reached through the cage, touching his forehead. She extended the knife and poked him with the handle. He grabbed her wrist, felt the knife and placed it in the waistband of his trousers. He held and kissed her hands, and then murmured, "I'll send for you, Milinda.

I'll come back and get you. I promise."

"There's a canvas bag under the cage. Use the codes and head to Canada. They say we can be free up there. Now get gone out of here."

"I'll send for you... I'll get you out of here. Go down by the fire and sidetrack them lackeys. I'll be gone in a minute."

Joshua hid behind the cage while Milinda approached the three guards, warming themselves by the fire.

"Why, hey there pretty missy," one of them remarked. "You be a lookin' for a new man now?"

Milinda knew that the one who spoke had a crush on her. She had fended off his advances before. She wrapped her arm around his waist, pressing her body close. She squeezed him lightly. "Could be a lookin' ... you might kin warm my bed sometime."

Madison cut easily through the rope latch and then paused. He listened to the murmur of voices, certain that Milinda held their attention. He slowly opened the bamboo cage door and slithered underneath the structure. He fumbled through the moist dirt and moss with both hands, finding the small bag and clutching it tightly. Slowly, he crawled on his stomach for a dozen yards. Finally enveloped in the foliage, he crouched, ran another hundred feet, and then stood erect. He climbed the rail fence and printed southward, taking the forked intersection in two leaps. In several minutes he was well south of the camp, heading down the road toward the Rhoades Plantation. He ran at a trot for about ten minutes, and then walked for five, rationing his strength. He had no idea of the time of night, but he wanted to put as much distance as he could put between himself and the Forks before dawn.

Back at the cage, Joshua crawled inside.

Not long afterward, a rooster crowed and John Armstead greeted Sheriff John Martin, a corrupt Woodville lawman who remained in office at the pleasure of men like Armstead and Bankston. He was an older man—some twenty years in his Natchez office protecting slave traders. "I hear you fixin' to have a hanging Mr. Armstead. What happened here last night?"

"'Come down from that horse... follow me. ...got a Negro boy locked up... he killed Isaac. Strangled him, by God."

"I'll be damned."

Sheriff Martin dismounted and together, he and the slave merchant walked toward the cages. Armstead explained the previous evening's murder of Isaac Bankston by the 'savage' slave. He said nothing about Rebecca and the Kentucky merchant.

"Hanging's too good for him," Sheriff Martin said. "Just whip him to death." Will you be taking over Isaac's holdings? I've got interests in—"

Armstead interupted, assuring him that nothing would change; he would continue the business and the sheriff's cooperation would be amply rewarded as it always had been. They rounded the corner by the pens. Several black trustees stood in front of an open cage, gawking. Joshua stood amongst them.

"He done slipped away, Massa'" one of them said. "Gone like a ghost outta' hell."

Armstead was livid. He called for a posse, dogs and the assistance of the sheriff. In a few minutes, four of Armstead's most trusted white overseers, Isaac Bankston's two bodyguards, and the sheriff were ready to depart. Armstead ordered that the cage guards be scourged immediately.

"Ten lashes might teach 'em something about guarding my property. I won't stand for no murdering Negro to get out from under me."

John Armstead stopped the posse at the door of the 'breeding pen'. From atop his horse, he called for Milinda and the others.

Milinda, Caroline, Elizabeth, Caleb, Matthew, and Joshua filed out and stood in a row outside the lodge. All but Milinda hung their heads low.

"I know ya'all had a hand in his escape. Who cut the ropes...? One of you give him a knife? Speak up!"

The group stood silent. Finally Matthew said, "we don't know, Massa'. We been shut up in here since the whuppin'. Ain't nobody been outside."

Armstead, clutching his whip, dismounted. He struck Matthew hard across the face, scaring him for life. "You damn Negroes know something. Talk or you'll all get the same."

Milinda stepped forward. She smiled and said. "Please don't whip us, Massa', I'll tell you what you want to know."

"Where'd he go... how long...?"

"I don't know how long he's been gone. He use to talk about New Orleans... gonna' catch a freedom boat, he said."

"Why, thank you, you lying black bitch. Do you think I'm stupid? You're his whore. No truth in you."

Armstead remounted. "We'll head north, pick up his trail along the road. He's probably headed up to Tennessee."

Sheriff Martin agreed: "We'll have him in an hour or two... have a hanging before the day is out."

Armstead looked at Milinda for a moment, and

then ordered that she be flogged with a leather flop. "Don't mark her up," he said. "I'll want her later." He leaned over in the saddle, staring into Milinda's eyes. "You'll rue the day you tried to deceive me."

They headed out of the gate at a gallop—their bloodhounds never given a chance to sniff out the trail—Armstead was so sure of Madison's direction. He led them north, along the road toward Memphis.

Madison put a mile between himself and the Forks, and then charged into the heavy forests. Thorns and branches tore at his flesh and at one point he fell into a slimy pool of stagnant water. It cooled him, but he was burning with fever and craved water. The surface of the pool lay thick with green scum. Balls of mosquitoes swarmed above it. Madison, desperate for fluids, spread the slime with his hands, sucking the dirty water into his scorching mouth and down his throat. He then turned his attentions to his aching body. He rinsed dozens of stinging red ant bites and picked off several bloodsucking leeches. He rested briefly against a tree, closing his eyes for several moments.

A hound bayed in the distance, startling him. He sprang upright, grasped his bag and continued to forge his way south, keeping the sun over his left shoulder and staying close to the road. He stepped out onto it when it appeared safe, increasing his stride. On short sections of road, he ran for a brief distance, and then dodged back into the forest at the slightest sound or flicker of movement.

At some point, he heard horses approaching and he made a mad dash back into the forest. He broke through thickets, wild berry bushes, poison sumac and heavy forest for almost a mile and in his haste, he lost all sense of direction. Out of breath, he now walked slowly through less tangled brush and thickets, soon finding himself in a jungle of virgin undergrowth. He had no idea of direction or any thought of what he might do next. He just walked, tearing away at tree limbs and foliage with his brute strength.

By mid-day, he was exhausted and lay prone upon a bed of palmetto leaves. He fell asleep for a few minutes, but was awakened by the sounds of barking dogs in the near distance. There was no mistaking the mission or intent of these animals. *Bloodhounds, I've got to get moving.*

Madison arose and bounded in a direction that offered the least resistance from the jungle he was lost in. In another half mile, he broke into a field; what appeared to be abandoned farmland. A decrepit wooden structure appeared on the horizon and he made a beeline for it. Somewhere near the entrance to the shack, he felt the earth beneath him give way and unable to stop himself, he fell, feet first into an abandoned well. He managed to grasp the upper ledge, breaking his fall somewhat, but he soon fell deeper into the narrow shaft. At the bottom, he stood in a foot of water and muck. A small rotting dead animal floated against his leg and came to rest against his trousers. It fouled the air and Madison fought the urge to gag and cough.

He was unable to see, but could hear the incessant barking of the hounds as they neared his unlikely hiding spot. Voices shouted commands to the dogs and loud pronouncements of possible hiding locations echoed nearby. Madison crouched deeper into the well. Soon, the dogs were above the hole, sniffing and baying, but could collect no scent above the stench of the rotting carcass. The loud banging of a door, and then cursing shouts of frustration rolled across the field. Madison began to breathe again when he realized that the search party was going away. He waited a full hour until he was satisfied that they had indeed, moved on.

Using his back as a brace against one wall of the well and his knees against the other wall, he inched his way upward. His strength was waning rapidly, but within twenty minutes, his head topped the rim of the shaft. He paused and looked around, making certain no one of the search party remained. With his last few ounces of strength, he pulled himself out and onto the ground. He lay there for a while and was soon dozing, no matter how hard he fought to stay awake.

Starving and nearly delirious from the lack of water, Madison lay there for several hours. Evening shadows rolled over him and before long, it was nightfall. In and out of consciousness during the night, he groaned a few times and shifted his position once or twice to avoid the insects that tried to feed on him. He was too exhausted to make a move of any significance. Somewhere during this moonless night, in his slumber, he felt a wetness come to light on his forehead and then against his cheek. Fearful that it might be a reptile or vermin of some sort, he lay absolutely still, but was fully awake. A rhythmic and damp lapping fell upon his face and Madison dared to open one eye. *Lord almighty, it's a dog, lapping at me like I was salt lick of some kind.*

Madison opened both eyes, studied the creature for a moment and surmised that it was a small dog of unknown breed. It was mostly white with black markings scattered across its fur; a Terrier perhaps. He rose to his knees, almost elated that he had some company; another living creature; a companion of sorts. He reached and gathered the animal to his breast, petting him and cooing soft words. Madison rolled onto his side and cuddled the dog into his armpit. Together they slept that way until early dawn.

Madison awoke with a start, his heart racing. He was famished and thirsty. He raised up on his knees, listened, observed, and then stood. There was a stillness to the air, and after a while he and the little dog, while running circles around his feet, approached the ramshackle building. Once inside, Madison saw that it had no value to him. The cupboards and shelves were bare, dusty and laden with cobwebs and mice droppings. He sank into an old wooden chair, the only furnishing in the place. He buried his face in his hands and prayed. The dog jumped into his lap, seemingly happy to have found a new master. "Go on, little dog," Madison uttered. "You picked the wrong man to tend to you. I can't do you any good."

The dog spring from his lap and raced to the open door. He spun in circles, arousing Madison's curiosity. He stood and approached the dog who then tore through the doorway and sprinted into the adjacent woods. "Well, that's the last I'll see of you, little gopher." He could hear the dog yapping as it made its way through the forest, the sounds growing fainter with each passing moment. Madison sat on the porch, wondering what he should do next. He was hungry and thirsty. Food and water become a near obsession.

It was only ten or fifteen minutes until the dog returned, bearing a freshly killed rabbit within its jaws. He dropped it at Madison's feet.

"Lord have mercy… you have answered my prayers." He took the warm and limp rabbit to the edge of the porch and withdrew Milinda's knife from his waistband. With a few deft strokes, he had the rabbit skinned and gutted. Next, he sought the items he would use to build a fire.

Friction-based fire making was a common skill around the slave pens that Madison had come to know. Flints and "Lucifer Matches" were scarce and slaves often built their fires by creating friction against dry tinder.

Madison searched for and found a short plank made of cedar. Into it he cut a vee shaped notch and a hollow depression next to it. Next he selected a dry limb made of oak. He sharpened a point, and broke it into a short pole of about eighteen inches in length to use as a spindle. He gathered dry grass, leaves, and bark for a tinder nest and began drilling. It took about twenty minutes of tirelessly rotating the spindle through his hands, but eventually, he saw the spark of an ember. Using the piece of bark as a vessel, he carried the ember to his small stack of dry leaves and twigs, all the while blowing on it. In moments, he had a fire. He smiled at his survival technique and it seemed as if the little dog did also. He wagged his tail in jubilation.

Madison kept the fire small, fanning the smoke in an effort to hide it. Using a long stick, he roasted the rabbit over the flame and after half an hour, he bit into his first meal in several days. It was not enough to satisfy his hunger, but he shared a hind leg with his new friend, whom he now called, "Gopher."

After they had consumed it all except the bones, Madison carried the refuse to the well and dumped it in. He now searched for water and found it in a wooden rain barrel sitting a few yards in the rear of the shack. He drank his fill and replenished his leather canteen. It was an hour before dusk and Madison decided to move at night, but he did not know in which direction to travel.

As if the little dog could read his mind, Gofer

trotted to the wood line and barked at Madison to follow. Without any other options, Madison followed. With little daylight left, they traversed thickly wooded but easy trails, probably left by the search party of the day before. Sometime during the night, they both slept, and dawn found them just a few dozen yards from the edge of a road. At Gopher's insistence, they made their way out to the road, but remain hidden within the trees.

The sun was high overhead when Madison heard, and then spotted, several wagons headed toward him. He and Gopher dove into the bushes and waited. Exhausted and demoralized, he didn't much care about the possibility of snakebite or any other perils hidden in this forest. His mouth was dry again, his water pouch was empty, and he was near collapse from running, off and on, for two days.

The approaching black waggoners were singing, chanting prayers actually, as they moved slowly along the road. Heavily laden and stacked high with grain, the wagons spilled a trail of seed behind them.

Madison unexpectedly felt hope spring from within him. He recognized the man driving the lead wagon. He was the old slave who had given him and Rebecca water and food on the march to Natchez. Madison waited until the wagons were almost upon him, and then leaped from the bushes, shouting, "Hey, ya'all, I need a little water... water, please."

The tugging mules paid little attention but heeded the commands of the lead driver, Amos Jefferson. "Whoa, Blue. Whoa, Biscuit," he said. The caravan of three wagons slowed to a halt, their drivers pulling on the reins.

"Who is you?" Amos asked. "You looks like trouble."

"My name is Madison Washington... need water,

just some water... Please."

Amos Jefferson, the aged and trusted slave of planter Elmer Rhoades, reached behind him for a skin of water. He threw it to Madison. "That's all I kin do fer' you, Boy. Take it and go. Runaway slave ain't nothing but worry. Are they 'a-hind you? Heard any dogs?"

Madison put the leather flask to his lips and swallowed half of the contents without stopping. "Thank you," he said. He tucked the drinking pouch into his bag. "... heard a Coon Dog a while back."

"Now, git up, Blue... Hey... git up, Biscuit," Amos Jefferson commanded the mules. He flexed the reins and the caravan started a slow forward motion. Madison walked alongside the lead wagon, unsure of what he might do next. Suddenly, he reached into his bag and pulled out the shawl—the codes—waving it at Amos.

Amos pulled hard on the reins. "Whoa, Blue... whoa, Biscuit." He turned and looked long at Madison. "Does I know you, boy? Seen you 'afore? You just come out the Forks?"

"Yes, Sir. You gave me and my mother food and water when we came along this road a while back. You prayed with us—"

Well, I'll be switched... You growed some, Boy. You sho' had a pretty momma."

Madison grew anxious standing in the middle of the road; the jungle forests were better concealment. He very quickly explained all that had happened, the murder of his mother and his escape a day or two before. Madison had lost track of time. "I'm going to Canada," he announced.

"Ah knows," Amos said. "Had to be sure it was you'. Lots o' runaways along these roads... bounty hunters 'a-hind 'em. Codes done it fer ya'. Your Momma dead, you say? ... rest her soul.""

Amos had already made his decision. He stood and waved the other drivers forward. There were five additional men in all: drivers and assistants. Amos gave them a few words of instructions. They grabbed wide grain shovels from their wagons and rapidly scooped out the barley from the center wagon onto the ground. When it was empty, it revealed a false bottom. At about six-inches above the floor base, a half dozen planks rested on wooden ridges, creating a crawl space that could barely accommodate a man of Madison's size.

Amos gave a series of quick commands to Madison. "Git in the hole. Wrap that piece a sailcloth 'round you self. It smell like onions... turnips... throws the dogs off. They's a hole big enough for breathing. Git up against the headboard... find the hole quick. Boys gonna' cover you up. Might be tight, stout like you is. Hey, Boy… you takin' that dog with you?"

"If I can, Sir. He saved my life."

"Well, I reckon he can ride up here with me. Go ahead and catch him, hand him up to me."

Madison reached for Gopher, but the little dog growled, put his tail between his legs and turned in circles. Madison spoke to him as if he were human, explaining that they had found an escape and had to hurry.

Gopher shook his head, looked at Madison for a moment and bounded back into the forest.

"Quick like, Boy… get in the wagon. That dog will be all right."

"Yes he sure will, Mr. Jefferson. He was an angel sent from God… there is no other explanation." Madison bounded into the wagon and rolled himself in the smelly tarp.

Amos directed him. "Whatever happens, say nary a word... no sound. You do, and we all gonna' hang."

Madison knew better than to ask any questions that could come later. He wrapped himself completely in the sailcloth and found the air hole. Immediately he felt shovels of grain being slammed onto the boards above him. In fifteen minutes, they were ready to move, the ground swept clean of all but a few kernels of grain.

Amos whistled and snapped the reins. "Git up, Blue! Git up, Biscuit!"

Chapter Sixteen

The Underground Railroad

The convoy ambled north for several hours, passing through Natchez as the sun began to fall in the western sky. Slaves were not allowed to stop in Natchez; a city ordinance prohibited it after a cholera outbreak some years before. They rode out of town, took the Alabama-Tennessee artery at the Forks of the Road, never turning their heads toward the slave pens. An early darkness fell around them and the skies ahead looked stormy. At about seven in the evening, they settled into a clearing and built a fire. Drinking a little water, they chewed on fatback and dried beef.

One man slipped under the wagon and stuffed jerky up to Madison through his breathing hole. With a bamboo straw, he provided several mouthfuls of water. "We sit here 'till just before daylight. You don't move or say nothing. If you praising Jesus like you do... do it in your head. And don't you worry none, brother Washington."

Madison grunted his acknowledgment. He had drifted into and out of sleep as the caravan moved north-ward. It helped to heal his wretched body and ease the pain of his scourging.

Daylight beckoned and Amos and his drivers prepared the mules to move. Blue began braying loudly, then Biscuit. Amos heard the approaching dogs first, and then the riders. He said nothing, waiting for the ultimate test of his clandestine operations: the Mississippi branch of the Underground Railroad.

John Armstead and the sheriff drew near, halting their horses directly in front of Amos. The remaining posse surrounded the wagons. The drivers stood by their mules, holding the reins.

"That you, Amos Jefferson? Where you headed with these wagons in the dark? Mr. Rhoades send you up this way?"

Amos Jefferson had been a slave all his life, born in the pens at the Rhoades plantation. An older man, about sixty-four, he had gained the trust of his master. He came and went as he pleased, often taking caravans of farm products to neighboring towns and states.

"Yes, Suh, Mr. Armstead. We be camped here all night. Lost a bit o' time with a dry axle yester'dee'.

"I said, where you headed?"

"Massa' Rhoades... he sendin' us up to Memphis. We's to pick up a load o' pitch to bring back. We need to git a move on."

Several members of the posse began probing the grain heaps with bamboo poles cut from alongside the road. The dogs circled the wagons, confused, baying and barking, but giving no sign of having picked up a human scent. Madison, faring well beneath the load, held his breath and listened.

Armstead leaned forward in the saddle. "You tell Mr. Rhoades that I deeply regret I had to inspect his loads but we have a runaway on our hands; a murderer. We figure he went north. You see a healthy boy wearing one of my uniforms along this way?"

"No Suh, Mr. Armstead. We been moseyin' along most of yester'dee'. Ain't seen nobody. He wouldn't be out on no road now, would he? Who'd he kill?"

"Guess you ain't seen nobody," Sheriff Martin said. "Hell, he killed Isaac.... It's all over the territory."

"My Lord have mercy! We's sorry to hear 'bout Massa' Bankston... now, he were a right good man."

One of the posse returned to the front. "Ain't nothing in these wagons, Mr. Armstead. Let's make camp and cook some grub. We been riding all day and night. Dogs need watered and fed."

"I didn't hire you to make decisions for me, Mister. We're riding back south toward the old King place. Maybe that little bitch was telling the truth. You sure there ain't nothing in them wagons?"

"Nothing but corn."

"Then let's get a move on."

Mr. Armstead turned to Amos. "I'll tell Rhoades everything was all right with ya'all."

"Yes, Suh, Mr. Armstead. My Massa' do worry 'bout us."

Within minutes the riders were gone and Amos Jefferson urged his mules into action. That evening they camped near Iuka, Mississippi, near the Tennessee and Alabama borders. They had taken seldom-used trails, avoiding the Natchez Trace and the many travelers that journeyed there. The following day they made their way into Memphis, pulling up before a black-owned feed and seed store on Mulberry Street. A middle-aged man stepped out onto the porch. "How many this time, Amos?"

"Three... two young bucks and a girl."

"Been long on the road?"

"Three days and nights."

"Get your wagons into the barn and dig them out... quick. They're probably half dead by now."

This was Amos Jefferson's twenty-second trip to Memphis. In three years he had delivered more than one hundred slaves to freedom.

Amos and his drivers followed the storekeeper's instructions and within minutes, three slow moving bodies emerged from beneath the grain, one from each wagon. Madison shook the loose kernels from his collar, dusted himself off and asked for water. The girl, Martha Pullman, looked weak, but after some fresh air and a pint of water, she recovered quickly. Ely Griffin was an ebony-smooth fellow of about eighteen. The journey had not affected him much. They shook hands, and then all three spontaneously embraced. It was as much a celebration of their achievement as it was a bonding—and a promise to each other that they would survive.

Amos pointed to the haylofts. "You kin make bed up there. Someone gonna' fetch ya'all food and water."

"Where are we, Mr. Amos? I need to get to Canada. We close to that?" Madison asked.

Amos laughed, shook his head and leaned back against a wagon. He chewed nonchalantly on a straw. "'Spose 'I kin tell you a bit, but if'n you knows too much, you might spill the milk... if'n you get catched."

Madison nodded. "I can keep a secret."

"Look at your codes. There be ten stops 'afore Canadee. You is in Memphis, Tenn-see; the first safe house out a The Forks. Couple days... someone come git ya'"

"Who?" Martha Pullman asked.

"I don't know who by name, but they be God-fearin' folk... Quakers, they calls 'em. They'll carry you on to Indianee, O-hee-ho, Pennsalvina, Sheekaygo, Dee-troit.... All 'da way up to Canadee."

Martha drew closer to Madison. "How many days will it take?"

"You be ridin' in wagons fer a time and you be hiding under crops again, maybe. Best I can tell you, it be a week 'afore anybody come fer ya'."

"Do we all three go together?" Ely asked.

"Look yonder." Amos pointed to the lofts. Almost a dozen black faces appeared from beneath the hay. "This be a right busy railroad," Amos laughed. "It gonna' get busier 'cause freedom come one day. Ya'all work for it and don't never lose hope." Amos and his drivers went into the store, spending the night there and moving on at daylight. They went farther into Memphis to pick up their return loads.

Madison managed to shake Amos' hand and say goodbye to each of the drivers before they left. He lay awake all night, praying for them and waiting to tell Amos about his plans for rescuing Milinda and Isaac.

"So you wanna' find yo' woman and boy, does ya'? Well, stay in touch, Son." Amos said. "I might kin help when that time comes."

Over the next several days, just as Amos had promised, food and water was delivered to the secreted former slaves. One by one, and sometimes two by two, they were beckoned out of their hiding places and disappeared. Both black hands and white arms helped pull them from the hay. On the seventh day after their arrival, a man's voice called out for Madison, Martha, and Ely. "Come down, we are departing straight away."

Madison was the first to crawl down the ladder. He was impatient to get moving; to get to Canada as fast as he could and then send someone for Milinda and little Isaac. At the bottom of the ladder, he could hardly believe his eyes. A white minister, dressed in a long black cassock and wearing a flat wide brimmed hat stood before him. He carried a Bible in one hand. They shook hands and he beckoned all three runaways into his covered wagon, a modern prairie schooner. They began their journey, unsure of where they were headed, but happy to be able to do so. The minister said very little except to explain that if they were stopped, to say nothing, he would do all of the talking. "Should someone ask you a direct question, do not answer. Appear ignorant or deaf. If the wrong word is passed—even a hint of what we are doing—we'll be shot on the spot; you can be sure of that."

"Who are you, Sir? Are you a man of the cloth... what faith?" Martha Pullman asked.

"I'm a gun thrower, lady... a bounty hunter. This business pays better. Don't let this 'get-up' fool you. I'm armed."

"Who pays you?" Madison asked.

"I told you that you don't need to know too much. They'll squeeze it out of you. Just know that them Jesus-loving Yankees think you're worth it. Now shut up."

Madison, Ely, and Martha complied and remained silent. The wagon continued plodding throughout the night and Madison could tell he was traveling northeast by the position of the stars. Charles King had taught him how to measure seven sections of the cup side of the big dipper and space them below the constellation's handle. There he would find the North Star and directly beneath that, the direction was always north.

At a way-station in Elizabethtown, Kentucky, their driver exchanged his tired horses for fresh ones. After taking on food and water, they were on their way again. At daylight on the fifth day, they crossed the Ohio River by barge and entered Indiana territory. They had not made a permanent camp at any time and were not challenged by highwaymen of any sort. By nightfall they were in a barn, in a hayloft, on the outskirts of Indianapolis. After consuming some dried corn and beef, they fell exhausted onto the hay. The gunslinger did not say good bye and he was not seen again. Madison assumed he returned for another cash crop of runaway slaves.

The owner of the farm and his wife proved to be much more congenial than their former driver. They were Quakers and members of the largest camp of abolitionists within their sect. They visited with the trio for several hours, explaining that the most perilous part of their journey, out of Mississippi, was over. They cautioned that bounty hunters still roamed the roads and they would have to stay in hiding. "From here, you will go in different directions to the destinations you asked for," the farmer said.

Ely Griffin would go on to Columbus, Ohio, in the morning and Martha Pullman to Pittsburgh the following day.

"You, Mr. Washington, shall get your wish. You'll leave for Detroit in a few days or more. From there, you can boat your way across the river to Canada. Good luck to all of you," the kindly Quaker said.

Madison's traveling companions were picked up at the appointed times and whisked away to their destinations. Madison waited for his call. After four days, a gentle voice summoned him in the middle of the night. His Quaker benefactor bid farewell and handed him the reins of a sturdy horse. He pointed at another horseman standing in the shadows. "Luther will take you the rest of the way."

"Thank you for your kindness," Madison said. The horse stirred and his mind flashed back to Charles King's riding lessons. He mounted and gained command of the steed, waiting on the man called Luther.

"You can handle a horse... Good." Luther said. "It will be much faster this way."

Madison rode side by side with Luther, observing him and speaking only when it was necessary. *Another bounty hunter, I suppose....*

Luther, a short, stocky man with speckled gray whiskers, spoke very little at first. He dressed in the cotton coveralls and gingham blue shirt of a planter, but wore the same strange looking wide-brimmed black hat Madison had seen so often at the Quaker farm. At daybreak they rested in a wooded area off the road and Madison tested Luther with a few questions. "How far is Detroit? How much does it cost to get me to Canada?"

"What do you mean? How much am I paid?"

"I guess that's what I mean. Why do you do it?"

"I hope to be paid very well, Son... in Paradise. Not everyone is in it for the money."

"Who are you?"

"My name is Luther Johnson, but that's not important. I am a Quaker. I have a Catholic friend in Canada. He'll be glad to see you."

"Quakers... Catholics..?" Madison queried. "I don't know about them. Why do they help us?"

"Although we are of a different race and faiths, Madison, we believe that all men are equal... entitled to God's protection."

"Your friend... he feels the same?"

"His is a rich parish... substantial holdings. They pay the costs... hire anyone willing to face the dangers."

"Is he like me... Negro?"

Luther laughed. "Not hardly. But we are all brothers in the eyes of the Lord. We have an obligation to Him to rescue as many souls as possible, African or otherwise."

"Can you get my wife and baby to Canada?"

Luther sighed. "No, Mr. Washington. There are more than seven-hundred thousand slaves in these United States and its territories. We can't possibly rescue them all."

Madison ached for Milinda and Isaac. He felt some guilt for having left them. "What will happen to them, to us?"

"God will send a trumpeter, and very soon. There will be a mighty battle. Much blood shall be spilt... but your people will be free."

"A battle...? Will you have to fight?"

Luther smiled. "No, I am a pacifist, a man of peace. The Catholics and the Protestants... even the Jews will fight for you. I serve the Lord in my own way."

Catholics, Protestants... never heard such names. I think I like this Quaker man. God is surely protecting me. Momma was right about Him showing up when you least expect it. Maybe He was Gopher.... Naw!

They reached the Detroit River at daybreak on the fifth day after leaving Indianapolis. Michigan was considered "free territory," Madison's guide explained. "But, be wary Bounty hunters comb these roads too. They'd like nothing better than to take you back to Mississippi."

Bold, but vigilant, they rode side-by-side along the Rouge and Raisin rivers.

Chapter Seventeen

Canada

Luther paid their passage and they boarded a flatboat at Belle Isle. In an hour, they had helped pole their way across the Detroit River and landed in Windsor, Ontario. A middle-aged man in a buggy was waiting among the small crowd on the shore. He stepped down and ran to Luther and Madison, warmly shaking their hands. "God bless you, Luther. You did it again. How was your trip?"

The man and Luther talked for a while. Madison waited patiently for them to finish, but his keen eye immediately captured the beautiful landscape of the North Country. His body felt a chill and he rubbed his arms for warmth. It was July, 1841. Mississippi seemed very far away. On a whim, Madison knelt and scooped up the sandy soil of his new country. He sifted it between his fingers, looked up, and gave thanks to God.

Luther soon departed and the man shook Madison's hand again. "I'm Charles Languois," he said. "Welcome to Canada, Mr. Washington." He explained that Madison could work on his farm for room and board, or until something developed for him. "Do you know how to handle animals... perhaps use a scythe?"

Madison appeared puzzled. "A little, I think.... Why do you ask?"

"We are wheat farmers."

Charles Languois was a trim and sinewy man of French ancestry. He wore his long black hair in a pony-tail, the length of it hanging well below the collar of his shirt. His rough hands and weathered face suggested many years of hard work in the cold Canadian winters. Despite his hardened appearance, he was a gentle man who appreciated the company of people. He and his wife, Nancy, had occupied their land north of Windsor for thirty years. They had no children and their few relatives lived in the distant provinces of Canada. Their home, nevertheless, was frequently occupied by guests. Itinerant laborers and farmhands were always welcome at their diner table. They loved people and they harbored no prejudices.

As his father had done before him, Charles raised wheat, barley, oats and hops for the breweries in Canada and in Detroit. Much of his harvest went into cities and towns along the Detroit and Ohio Rivers, supplying bakeries and manufacturers as far south as Louisville, Kentucky. Farming proved to be a profitable business for the Languois and they had become extremely wealthy over the years.

Charles and Nancy gave all credit for their prosperity to the Lord, and they began and ended each day on their knees, praising God and giving thanks for his blessings. Charles attended St. Isadore Catholic Church in Detroit, where he had been baptized almost fifty years before. Each Sunday, or as often as necessary, he rode a paddle-launch or helped pole a ferry across the river to Detroit. Charles was an active member and leader of several committees in his church, one of which brought slaves out of bondage through the Underground Railroad. It was an expensive undertaking and Charles supported the effort with his pocketbook. Many of the freed slaves had found new lives through his sponsorship.

Madison, somewhat bewildered at this new station in life—so far removed from the agony of the whipping post and the misery of slavery—took a moment to query Charles. "A scythe? Do you mean for cutting crops?"

"Yes, we have some modern implements, but most of the wheat is harvested by scythe and sickle."

"I didn't do field work as a slave, but I can learn. My daddy worked a scythe. I watched him as a boy."

"What trade, what skills do you have?"

"I can read and write."

Charles laughed. "Well, now…that is something."

"I won't disappoint you, Massa' I'll do what I have to—"

Charles put a hand on Madison's shoulder and doffed his straw hat with the other.

"Madison, please do not use that word ever again. There is only one master, and you well know it. Call me Charles."

"Yes, ah… Charles. I'll repay ya'all someday."

"You owe us nothing, but your help will be appreciated. We're facing the biggest harvest we've had in years. I trust that your father taught you well."

Madison was filled with a growing sense of optimism, a hope that had been buried in his soul all of his young life. Although he had enjoyed the privileges of a favored slave in Charles and Ruth King's household, he was still a slave there, and he knew it. Here in Canada, listening to his new friend and benefactor, he actually felt free for the first time in his life and the sensation was overpowering. "I'll work mighty hard for you, Sir. I'm real strong."

"You appear to be—"

"If I can plant my roots, I'll have my family here with me before too long. We'll get a small plot and farm wheat and corn... just like you do." Madison clapped his hands, danced a few steps, and gave Charles the broadest of smiles.

Charles took Madison by the arm and they mounted the buggy. They rode north through the countryside for more than an hour. It seemed to Madison that Canada was just one big grain field. For as far as his eyes could see, acres and acres of wheat rippled gently against the cool wind. They passed farmhouses and barns, white and blue, appearing as if they had been freshly painted that day. People looked up from their work and waved to them as they rode by. Madison waved back, shouting, "Hey, Ya'all!" Freedom was an exhilarating experience for him and he was adapting to it well.

Charles Languois asked Madison about his family. "Tell me about your wife and child... your past. I can hardly imagine being a slave."

Madison seemed to have found a new voice. He babbled to Charles, telling him all about Rebecca, Milinda, and little Isaac. He described his years on the King plantation, Miss Agnes, Rufus Bohlinger, and his abrupt deliverance into the slave pens at the Forks of the Road. He told Charles about his mother's murder and his subsequent whipping and escape. "I'm a renegade now.... I killed a man. Maybe you won't want me here—"

"The authorities are after you?"

"I'm sure they are."

"You tell a tragic story, Madison. No harm will come to you here. Mississippi law does not apply. Pray on it and ask for God's forgiveness."

Madison found Charles Languois to be an eager listener and he poured out his soul to him. Something he thought he'd never do with a white man. He made it clear that any future he might have must include Milinda and little Isaac.

"Perhaps in time, we can do something for your wife and child, Madison."

"When?"

"We'll be holding a committee meeting very soon. Can you tell me where Milinda and Isaac are? Possibly we can rescue them. No promises..."

Charles and Nancy Languois showed Madison to a room in the upper loft of their home. It was comfortably furnished and had a window where Madison could view the stars and think about his Milinda and Isaac. He was invited to take his meals with Charles and Nancy, use all of their home's facilities and share in "God's blessing's," as Nancy made clear. Prejudices were nonexistent in this home and Madison sensed it. Charles made no demands on Madison except asking that he join them for evening prayers—which he gladly did.

On a cool morning of his second day at the Languois farm, Madison and Charles ventured out into the barns and then the grain fields. Mild breezes bowed the tops of the wheat, to and fro, making them appear golden and alive in the early sun. It was a breathtaking scene with wheat blossoming "straight up into the sky" as Madison described what he saw to Charles. He sensed freedom boiling deep within him and he wished that Rebecca had lived long enough to share it with him. "Milinda and Isaac will see this all someday."

Later that morning Charles approached him holding a scythe. Madison recognized the mowing tool and
visualized it in his father's strong hands. He had never
held one, but eagerly took the implement from Charles.

"During harvest, I'll hire nearly a hundred men to
cut and shock the wheat. They come from all over Canada
and the United States."

"Shock the wheat...?"

"Yes... stack and tie the bundles."

"They use slaves in Mississippi."

"Pity.... It is work a man should take pleasure in."

"Teach me to use the big blade... the scythe."

"Exactly what I was thinking," Charles agreed.
"Master this tool and you master the truth of God's gifts...
laboring in the fields. Let me show you how."

Charles grasped the short handle of the curved
pole with his right hand, holding the top with his left. He
spread his feet, bent slightly at the knees, and then made
several wide swings with the blade. His motions were
smooth, powered by his shoulders and waist. Charles handed the tool to Madison. "See, it's easy. Wet your palms...
helps your hands stick to the wood... hardens the calluses."

Spitting on his hands seemed odd to Madison.
He rubbed the moisture over his palms and grasped the
scythe. "It does feel tight."

"Ride it as you would a horse. Make it do the
all the work."

Madison adopted a stance much as Charles had
done. He rotated to the right, coming back to the left in a
wide arc, holding the blade just above the ground. Wheat
stalks fell in ragged clumps as Madison drove the tip of the
blade into the ground on his first swing. He and Charles

laughed. "You let it run away from you, Madison. Balance is the key."

"I'll get the feel of it." He took another stroke, smoother this time. After a half dozen attempts, Charles interrupted him with a bit more advice then left him alone to practice. Later that day, Madison was cutting the grass in front of the Languois home. Nancy told Charles that it looked as if "it were sheared with a pair of scissors."

Charles peered through the window, watching Madison work. "He's a fine young man. He has suffered much, but he has a certain spirit... learns very quickly."

That evening after supper and prayers, Charles beckoned Madison to sit on the large sofa, between he and Nancy. Madison hesitated, then accepted the offer.

"Do you enjoy tobacco... smoke a pipe, Madison? Perhaps you'd like a glass of brandy."

Madison stammered: "Mr. Charles... no disrespect... but in Mississippi... why, a white man would not touch my hand. You and Miss Nancy... this is not easy to get used to."

Nancy grabbed Madison's hand, covering it with both of hers. "So, it is our flesh... our difference in color that troubles you? Madison, you know your bible and you therefore know that God made us all in His unique image."

"The slaver uses the bible to justify his evil."

Nancy smiled, gently shaking his hands. "What is color, Madison? ...a science question..."

Madison thought about Miss Agnes for a moment. "A reflection of light."

"Exactly! Is it anything else?"

"No."

Their discussions carried well into the night, Nancy offering many pearls of insight into the issues of race and slavery. Charles talked of politics, economics, and religion. Madison's knowledge and view of the world and its peoples broadened beyond measure that summer evening in Canada.

Before going to bed, Charles outlined other chores that Madison could do to earn his keep. Madison said that he was better acquainted with the tasks of caring for livestock, and Charles Languois had many animals to tend. Charles told Madison that he'd be busy from early morning until dark if he accepted that chore.

"I'd like that," Madison said.

"You say you can read and write," Charles commented. "Would you like to pen a letter to your family? One of our riders might get it through."

Madison took the offered pen and paper to his room. He had not written anything for a while and was ashamed at the lettering he now used. He wanted the solitude of his room, the stars, and the inspiration of his mother to write. After some study, he slowly printed his message to Milinda.

My Dearest Milinda and Fine Son Isaac,

As I take my pen in hand, I am at rest after a long journey. My heart aches deeply for you. I am joyed to tell you that I arrived safe in Canada just a few days past. God took me through perilous places on my travels, but He holds me snug to his loving bosom. I am in the house of kind planters. His name is Mr. Charles Languois and his wife is Nancy. They are God-fearing people who make no wickedness to our people. I do not call him Master. I labor on their farm and have faith that we can make some future for you and Isaac. Mister Charles will get this letter to you and make passage for you on the freedom road.

You will be tested, but trust God and those who can help you. Call on Mister Amos Jefferson. He will send you and our little one into my loving arms. Write back your plans and tell me where Rebecca rests. Did you pray over her? Come to me, my love.

Madison.

At daybreak, Madison raced down the stairs, taking them two at a time. He offered the letter to Charles and Nancy to read.

"Your communiqué is touching, Madison. I can promise you nothing, but I will carry the letter to Detroit tomorrow. It will go south by a dispatch rider."

"How long will it take?"

"You left her at the Forks, you say? If God wills, it will find its way into Milinda's hands soon enough."

"Then what?"

"If we find her... learn her situation, perhaps we can add her name to the list. It is a long, long list."

Madison thanked him and went to the barn. He forked heaps of hay to the livestock, watered them and then vigorously set about cleaning stalls. The work provided some release of the guilt he felt for having left Milinda and Isaac. He was glad he had written the letter, his first. It was as if he were actually speaking to Milinda. He worked steadily for several hours, daydreaming of the life he would share with her and his son.

The following morning and every morning for the next several weeks Madison rose before dawn, fed the livestock, gathered eggs, practiced with his scythe and otherwise made himself useful. After each trip that Charles took to the shores of the Detroit River, Madison asked him if he had heard anything. A month slipped by, then two. It was harvest time; September 1841, and Madison grew

more anxious and despondent. On a mild and sunny afternoon, while currycombing the horses, Charles Languois
approached him. He held forth an envelope.

"Something for you, Madison. A message from
Amos Jefferson. It came by rider just last night."

Madison took the envelope, carefully unsealed
its edges, removed the paper and unfolded it. He looked at
Charles' sober face. "Something is wrong, isn't it? Please....
You read the letter for me, I can't seem to see the words."
Madison handed the letter to Charles and wiped his eyes.
His heart raced against a familiar rage now surging through
his veins.

Charles read aloud: "dear madison. your letter
to Milinda was told to me by mister amos who come up
this way. he is writtin it for me. milinda and isaac bin sold
to maccargo. they bin gone a bit. caroline gone and i all
whats left. man what buy em tradin in virginee. You find
em thar. rebecca is restin aside yore daddy and we prayed
and singed over her and laid a stone on her head. fare thee
well. elizabeth and amos."

Madison was stunned. His knees buckled and he
fell to shameless weeping. Charles attempted to comfort
him, but to no avail.

"Get up, Madison... it'll be all right..."

Madison stood suddenly, turned his back to
Charles, and then walked deep into the wheat fields. He
did not return for the night. In the morning, he approached
the house coming out of the rising sun. Nancy watched
him from her kitchen window. She called to Charles and
mentioned that he looked towering: "An angry Goliath
with something very grave on his mind."

Madison strode into the kitchen where Charles
and Nancy sat with their heads bowed in prayer. "I have

something to say," he announced.

Nancy quickly arose and put her arms around his neck. "Oh, Madison, we are so sorry. We are praying. There is always hope."

Madison pulled her arms away and held her at the wrists. "Hear me!"

"What is it, Madison?" Charles asked.

"I am going to Virginia... to get my family."

"Patience, Madison. Let us work on it"

"I cannot wait. It is time to break stone."

Charles sighed. "I see your determination. But let me contact some friends, see what they can do. There is time—"

"No.... It may be too late now! Every slave in Mississippi has heard of Thomas McCargo. He buys and sells quickly, shipping slaves all over the south. I must move fast. Will you help me?"

"If you go back there alone you could be captured and become a slave once more, Madison," Charles advised. "You would be going the wrong way on the railroad. It isn't structured to run from north to south."

"I'll go alone, without the railroad. I must get to them now. If they are sold again, I may never find them."

"All right, Madison, I'll talk to the church leaders. Perhaps we can arrange something. Perhaps nothing..."

"Today?"

"Well, I was thinking more like tomorrow. It is getting a little late to travel to Detroit and back."

"Today, Sir... please."

Charles packed a small bag. Madison harnessed a team of horses to his buggy and Charles climbed aboard. "With any luck, Madison, I'll be at St. Isadore's by late afternoon. Let's hope someone will sympathize with a crazy Freeman who wants to go South." Charles shook his head and snapped the reins.

Father John Coyle, the Rector of St. Isadore's, opened the door of his office, greeted Charles and asked him the purpose of his unexpected visit. "Sit down, Charles. I was just having tea. ...care for a cup? I'll pour. What brings you to church so late in the day?"

Charles accepted both offers and between sips of the hot brew, he explained Madison's wish to return to the south and find his wife and child.

"He's mad," Father Coyle said. "We don't have contacts running that way. He'd be caught as soon as he crossed the Mason-Dixon. All that effort and expense in getting him here... for nothing."

Charles made his best effort. "He's far from crazy, John. He's determined—more resolute than any man I've ever met. He might even succeed. I'd like to help him."

"You're a bit daft, too, Charles. If you encourage him, you'll have his fate on your hands. How do you feel about that?"

"If he is willing to take his chances at rescuing his wife and child, I will accept the responsibility for having sent him."

"It's out of the question."

Charles weighed the situation in his mind and concluded that Madison Washington, if anybody could, would indeed rescue his family. He deserved the chance.

Charles set his tea aside. "I'll more than finance the effort, Father. What do you say?"

Father Coyle studied Charles Languois, his largest contributor to the faith. "You know my weakness, Charles. There is the mortgage on the church."

"I'll take care of it."

Father Coyle broke into a smile. "All right, Charles, you win. I'll make some contacts this evening. We have several men... not the most religious types, you understand. But someone will take this gamble for pay. See me early tomorrow morning. Bring your Madison Washington with you."

Chapter Eighteen

Virginia

By nine o'clock the next morning, Charles and Madison were knocking on St. Isadore's rectory door. Father Coyle's housekeeper let them in. She led them to a sitting room and poured coffee. Father Coyle entered in a few minutes with an oddly dressed, tall man following him. His reddish hair and goatee beard made him appear notable, but his buckskin breeches and the large knife strapped to his waist made him look like something altogether different: tough, with frontier savvy. Madison was impressed.

Charles and Madison stood up. "Good morning, Father," Charles said. "This is Madison Washington."

The priest extended his hand. "You look every bit the reckless chap that I assumed you to be, Mr. Washington. You are also as impressive, physically, as Charles described."

"Thank you,"

"I'm told that your feelings for your family are about equal to your size... sometimes emotions cloud our judgment. This ill-advised foray into the south could be the end of you. " Father Coyle paused for effect. He wanted Madison and Charles to understand that what they were attempting was a risky endeavor. It could undermine all of their efforts at freeing slaves if it backfired.

"This is Mr. William Smith," Father Coyle said, pointing to his leather-clad companion. "He's the only man available to do what you ask. He's skilled at tracking and he knows the roads in and out of Virginia. He is also costing our congregation a lot of money, so you both had better make it back here... with your family."

William Smith extended his hand and smiled at Madison. "We'll make it, Padre, and return your investment... three new souls for the church."

William Smith was a tall lanky man, well over six-feet. A hank of blonde hair hung over his forehead, almost concealing his crystal blue eyes. Although he was middle-aged, he appeared to be well fit and exuded an air of confidence about their mission. William took charge and outlined a simple plan for getting Madison into Virginia. After loading ample provisions onto their horses, he and Madison bid farewell to Charles Languois and Father Coyle. Outfitted with a fine horse for the ride, he and William rode south along a wide dirt street, Gratiot Avenue. From there, they found the main road to Toledo, Ohio. They camped in a forest of white birch and maple trees that first night. The cool fall air chilled them and William began to collect firewood. He asked Madison to break out the dried fish and flour from his saddlebags. "Then gather leaves for bedding," he said.

Madison had no patience for the overnight delay and he expressed his desire to move on without a break. "If we keep riding, we can get there much faster. I don't need any rest."

"I'm twelve-years on the Santa Fe trail, Madison. Slow and steady wins the race."

"But they could be moving right now. I won't find them sitting around a campfire."

"There is danger at every step along these trails. Our best chance for success is to be alert and functional when we enter the slave holding states."

Madison reluctantly accepted William's logic. He helped build a small fire and after eating, they sat around the dying embers discussing what they'd do next.

"We'll be doing enough night riding when we hit Virginia," William said. "We go in and out as quickly as we can. Tell me, what do you know of the McCargos... from where do they do their dirty work?"

Madison poked at the ashes with a stick, deep in thought, trying to recall what he knew of McCargo's operations. "Men I knew on the King plantation came through McCargo's hands. My momma and daddy came through those pens. I was born in a McCargo horse stall."

"Did they ever talk about it?"

"I think my mother mentioned Richmond once or twice."

Madison stretched out on the colorful leaves and leaned his head against his saddle. He closed his eyes and tried to remember. He bolted upright after a few moments. "He uses ships to send his slaves to New Orleans. Daddy talked about the dark belly of a brig... out of Richmond or someplace. Hampton, I think it was."

"If McCargo transports slaves by sea, he'd have to have a holding area near the port of Hampton. I've been there. We'll head for Richmond, first. Maybe we'll pick up more information along the way."

Madison and William rolled up in blankets but remained awake and talked at great length that evening, building a familiarity with each other's past. William confessed that although the remuneration provided by the abolitionists was much better than he received scouting for wagon trains; in recent years, he had become a believer in the cause. "There will be a struggle over this issue, Madison, but slavery will end. There is great political pressure to abolish it."

"I didn't know."

"Why, even England and their territories do not hold for slavery anymore. Our country is young, destined to forge its future through blood."

"England?" Madison asked. "They don't have slaves? Where is this place called England?"

William explained a bit of the history of the United States. He told Madison about the revolution and George Washington. He briefly described the American system of government, the Congress, and named the presidents. William chuckled. "You have the fourth and first president's names, Mr. Madison Washington. You have a lot to live up to."

"My name is Bula Matadi."

"What? What sort of name is that?"

"African... My mother called me by that name."

"Interesting. Does it have meaning?"

"Breaker of Stone. It is my destiny, she said."

"I see... breaker of stone. I rather like the sound of it. Suggests great strength... optimism. Let's hope she was correct."

William answered Madison's many questions and explained that England, America's perpetual antagonist, had recently abolished slavery. "In fact, they don't hold for it in their colonies, island nations, or anywhere else."

"England sounds like the place for me. Where are these islands?"

"Great Britain has colonies all over the world. Some in the Bahamas, not far from our shores."

"Bahamas?"

"Yes, English islands. The Africans who reside there are British citizens... free..."

Madison listened in awe of William. His knowledge of the geography of the world and his explanations of history captivated him. He told Madison about the west and other places where men lived free. "There's Liberia, founded by free blacks and now a growing democracy. Then there is Canada and Mexico, although I don't recommend you live there." William Smith said.

"Why not"

"Bad government... bad water. Stay in Canada."

"Liberia... Bahamas..." Madison said. A plan was forming in his mind. He rolled over, placed his head on his saddle and said, "Good night."

Before daylight they were on the trail again. In two days and nights of riding, they were camped on the outskirts of Washington, D.C.

"We won't ride in broad daylight anymore," William told Madison. "We may be near the capital of democracy, but they turn their head to slavery."

"Where do we go next?"

"We're about to enter Virginia, the biggest slave state of all. After dark, we'll go straight from here and ride very quietly to Richmond. There's plenty of slave pens there."

"Where do you think they'll ship from?"

"I'm betting the port at Hampton... not too far down the James River from Richmond. It's a hotbed of buying and selling slaves."

Madison moved to unsaddle their horses, but William stopped him. "We stay ready to ride. As soon as it's dark, we go... take the main road for a while. Come day-light, we'll get off the roads and pick our trail through the forest. If we are approached by anyone, conceal yourself."

"And if they come up on us?"

"I'll tell them I'm a bounty hunter and I'm bring-ing a runaway slave back to the owner. You'll have to play the part, anything can happen." William checked his pistols and rested against a mound of earth. He closed his eyes, chewing on a straw. In a few moments, he sat straight up. "You could be captured, Madison... returned to slavery. We could both be shot. Do you still want to risk it?"

Madison explained once again about his love for Milinda, Isaac, Rebecca, and his life of slavery. He spoke with such passion that William did not question his determination further. Even if he had to live in slavery, Madison would be close to those he loved.

"Get some rest," William said. "If she is all that beautiful, we're sure to find her."

At sunset that evening they mounted their horses and rode hard toward Richmond. Near daylight, at the outskirts of the flourishing city, they rode into a thicket and made camp. William told Madison to stay concealed; he would ride ahead and try to gather information. Shortly before noon, he returned.

Madison was on edge. He was close to finding Milinda and Isaac, he knew, but his future was in William's hands. "What did you learn... anything?"

"You're in luck, Madison. I stopped at several

farms along the road... told them I was a buyer. Thomas McCargo and his son do most of the slave trading in these parts. They have acreage near Halifax, but they don't farm. They just buy and sell slaves... like cattle."

"Where... did you ask about Milinda—?"

"They have a holding pen no more than a few miles from here."

"Let's go!" Madison began saddling his horse.

"Not so fast, Madison. There are bounty hunters everywhere. You'll be my captured runaway from here on. I'll have to bind you."

"Tie my hands? Well, all right."

William continued. "When we near the pens, we'll part company. You'll have to find Milinda on your own. I'll wait three days and nights for you right here. Then I'm off to other places. I'll inform the church by letter or messenger"

"Agreed," Madison said. "If you get me to McCargo's place, I'll take it from there."

William tied Madison's hands in front of him after he had mounted. He took the reins of their horses and with Madison trailing, they rode slowly toward the McCargo slave complex, about five miles east of Richmond. They had barely traveled a mile, when rounding a curve in the road they were approached by two riders. They had no chance to conceal themselves.

"Hey, all," the lead rider said. He held up his hand as a signal for William and Madison to stop. Both riders were armed.

"Where you headed, Mister... with that slave?"

"He's mine. I caught him up near Ohio."

"Oh, you a bounty hunter, are ya'? You taking' him back to his Massa'?"

"That's right."

"And where might that be?"

"North Carolina."

"Where in North Carolina?

"Raleigh."

They sat still, in cold silence, measuring each other. The rider pulled back the hem of his black leather coat, exposing his sidearm. His squinty eyes stared at William.

"That's mighty fine, Mister. 'Cept you a stretch too far east to be making it for Raleigh. Who's the owner?"

"Carson... James Carson," William lied.

The second rider, the larger and grizzliest of the two, looked quizzically at William. He placed his hand on a musket tied to the horses flank. "Carson... never heard a no Carson in them parts. Now... where you think you going with that Negro?"

William recognized the hostility of the men. He turned his horse sideways, a tactic designed to minimize injury from a bullet. He drew back his own coat and placed his hand on his pistol. "I don't answer questions, boys. Get out of my way."

"Ya'all don't haf-ta' get uppity, Mister. We's lookin' for runaways, that's all."

"This boy is mine... money to me."

The larger horseman spoke. "McCargo pays a hundred dollars for every one we bring in. You can do the same. You can pass... didn't mean no harm."

William turned his horse to face the men and poked the steed in the ribs. He and Madison rode slowly past them when suddenly they drew their pistols and fired a volley, hitting William in the back of his head, neck, and spine. He was dead before he hit the ground. Madison wailed the mournful cry of a free spirit, now trapped and stripped of all hope. The highwaymen dragged William Smith's body off the road and threw it into the brush, not bothering to conceal it further. "Wild hogs can have 'em."

Without speaking, one rider grabbed the reins of Madison's horse and they rode at a gallop toward Thomas McCargo's infamous slave compound. In thirty minutes they pulled up in front of a vast array of low buildings, similar to those Madison had known at the Forks of the Road. Theophilus McCargo came out of a small house and met them. The sun was high in the sky, blazing hot, withering McCargo's white cotton suit. He held his hand at his brow, shading his eyes.

"What ya'all bring me, boys?"

The two marauders dismounted. "Found this runaway Negro up the road, "The big man said.

"He's stupid... don't speak, so we don't know where he come from. You can have him for a hundred," the other rider offered.

"Give ya' fifty."

"Where's your daddy? He pays a hundred."

Theophilus McCargo was a young, impetuous man. By twenty-three, rich foods and lazy living had made him grossly obese. He obeyed the dictates of his father, Thomas, and seldom made a worthwhile decision on his own. "Pa gone to Hampton. He got cargoes going south.... I'll take the slave."

Theophilus reached into the vest pocket of his long coat, withdrew some bills and handed them to the riders. "There's seventy-five for the slave and twenty-five for his horse and saddle. Ya'all get on back up the road. Find another one."

Theophilus watched the riders disappear into the

dust. He grabbed the reins of Madison's horse and led him to a corral where a dozen other black men lounged in the hay. Guards untied him and threw him inside. Madison stumbled and fell to his knees. The slaves hardly stirred; they were so accustomed to rude treatment. One man offered Madison some water, which he eagerly accepted.

"I'm Alfred Bird," he said, offering his hand. "Welcome to McCargo's slave paddock. You got a name?"

Madison introduced himself and told the story of his brief experience with freedom and his search for his family.

"Boy, you mean you were free and you came back into shackles? You gotta' love that woman... or maybe you're touched in the head," Alfred said.

While he spoke, the magnitude of what he had done swept over Madison. For the first time since he had thought of the idea he felt some uncertainty. Several other men sat up and listened to Madison's story. James Bruce, a lad about Madison's age, explained that these were temporary holding corrals. "We be shipping to New Orleans right soon."

Ben Blair, a small teenager, interrupted. "You are part of it now. ...think you're gonna' like New Orleans?" He slapped his knee and laughed.

Madison shot him a glance that said he hadn't come to these pens to be mocked. He asked where the women were kept, describing Milinda and explaining that she might have a small child in tow. "Anybody seen her... anyone look like that?"

"Women are kept separate... sheds out in back," Alfred answered. "No sense looking 'cause most of them left for Hampton two days ago. I ain't seen anybody like you say. Hell, ain't nobody that pretty."

Andrew Bankhead lay prone in the hay. He listened and then stirred. "I seen a gal like you say... had a small boy with her. I kinda had my own eye on her sweet self."

Madison perked up. "Where is she now?"

"I reckon she left with the first group. If it's her, she's in Hampton now. Who knows where to after that."

Madison was encouraged with the news that someone might have seen Milinda, but he was equally concerned that she and Isaac might already be at sea. He spent the afternoon and evening becoming acquainted with the other men and gleaning information about the impending trip to Hampton. He learned that Thomas McCargo assembled groups of forty or more slaves in a package and gathered them at Hampton near the docks. Other slavers brought in their human chattel and joined the packet there. When a ship was fully loaded, they sailed to New Orleans. An assemblage of slaves had been underway for the last week.

"We all are fixin' to go to Hampton come daylight," James Bruce said. "Maybe you'll find ya 'all's lady. One way or the other, you is going to New Orleans."

Theophilus McCargo counterfeited new registration papers on Madison. He called him into the headquarters building just before dark and interrogated him. Madison was noncommittal except to give his name. He said nothing of his recent past, his taste of freedom, or of his mission here. As William Smith had explained, the less he spoke, the more apt he was to be taken for an uneducated man—just another ignorant slave.

Theophilus McCargo dismissed him to the corrals, telling him to prepare for the march to Hampton at first light. Madison retuned to the enclosure, continuing his conversations with the men there. He held a council of sorts, describing an idea taking shape in his head. To rescue Milinda and Isaac, he would need help. After some discussion, Madison persuaded several of the men to join him in an escape attempt, or at least turn their backs while he did it.

Alfred Bird stood up. He shook his head and spit into the straw. "You fixin' to get us all whipped, maybe get yourself killed. Slave uprisings don't ever work out."

Madison studied Alfred and the others. He'd need all the help he could muster. "Have you heard of the Amistad, two years ago? Cinque?"

"You talking about that Spanish ship? It been whispered here and there, but I thought it was just a story."

"They were coming from Africa.... Cinque led a mutiny... took the ship. The government set them all free."

"How you know all this?" James Bruce asked.

"Trail rider, Mr. Smith.... He told me the facts. They all went back to Africa. We can do the same."

"Don't know about that," Alfred said.

"Trust me, we can do it," Madison argued.

"Hell, why not?" A slave named Ben Johnson, said. "Got nothing else to do. I'm in."

Several others agreed to participate, but just as many opposed it. "I don't care to hang just yet," Alfred Bird said.

Chapter Nineteen

The Road To Hampton

Madison spent a sleepless night on the straw. Before daylight, he and the remaining McCargo slaves were ordered onto the rutted and dusty road that led to Hampton. Each man carried one bag of personal belongings. Iron bracelets were snapped around the ankles of each slave, chaining them together in pairs and trios. Madison cringed at the sound and feel of metal around his ankle. Mounted horsemen rode up and down the line spinning and snapping their whips, confirming their authority over the slaves. The order to move came in a few minutes. An overseer called out: "Stir your black bones! Up with ye! Lag behind and you'll taste hot rawhide!"

Madison and the assembly of manacled humanity moved slowly forward. It took some adjustment, but they learned to walk with the shackles. The chains were long enough to be carried at the center, keeping them from dragging on the ground. Andrew Bird and Madison were bound together. The slaves were forbidden to talk as they moved along, but concealed by the dim early light, they whispered short comments to one another, never looking at the other man.

"I bet you feel like a fool now, Washington," Andrew said. "You were free and you came back."

Madison's faith in what he was planning to do was now unshakable. "I'm no fool, Andrew. I'll be free again and this time I'll have Milinda and Isaac with me."

"Freedom, freedom, freedom," Andrew mocked. "That's all you talk about. How you going to get free?"

Madison gathered the chain he was carrying with Andrew, drawing them closer together. "We'll be aboard a ship soon. There will come a chance... we'll rise up."

"And if you fail? Do you know what will happen to you... to all of us?"

"Are you afraid of freedom?" Madison asked.

They stumbled along for a while under the suspicious stares of the mounted overseers. The guards rode back and forth along the line of slaves shouting orders and nudging slaves into line with their horses. If someone stumbled or fell, other slaves were required to carry him. During one such commotion, Andrew found an opportunity to reply to Madison's question. "I'm not afraid of freedom. It is in my bones just as it burns in the soul of all Africans. At McCargo's place, a year ago, we broke for freedom."

"What happened?"

"No sooner did someone throw down his pitchfork and raise his voice and dozens of overseers rose up out of the fields like locusts. They formed a line and rode into us, shooting and cracking whips. There were too many of them. They know we long to be free and they watch us like rattlesnakes watch over their eggs."

"You took part in a McCargo revolt?"

"I'll show you the scars—"

"I'm sorry," Madison said. "But the whip won't stop us this time. At sea, we'll outnumber the guards and they won't have horses. The farther we get from land, the easier it will be. Join me, Andrew."

"Maybe. We'll see... What's your idea?"

Madison briefly outlined his plans to Andrew.

"Might work," Andrew said. "If it don't, what have we got to lose? Guess I'll toss my hat in."

Madison and Andrew spoke occasionally with other slaves as they trudged along the road. By nightfall, seven men had agreed to participate in the plot. Near the end of the first day they had covered about twenty of the ninety-miles to Hampton. Madison realized that it would take several days to get there after he learned the distance. He used the time to scheme and lay his escape plans with his fellow conspirators. They made camp at night and built small fires to cook and warm themselves. The slave masters provided adequate food and water, wanting their merchandise to be hearty looking upon arrival at the docks.

On the morning of the fifth day, the coffle of slaves crested a hill overlooking Hampton harbor. They stopped robotically, breathless at the sight of the sea and ships resting against the docks. Few of them had ever seen the ocean or sailing vessels such as these.

With a bright morning sun in his eyes. Madison squinted, scanning all of this magnificent harbor. His eyes came to rest on a particular ship where men scurried about loading provisions and heavy cargo aboard.

"What has your eye, Madison?" Andrew asked..

"Look there... that ship... it makes ready to sail."

"I see... what do the big letters say?"

"Creole."

Chapter Twenty

The Brig Creole

The American brig Creole, built in 1840, was commissioned at the port of Richmond, Virginia, on November 14. She was ninety-five feet long; twenty-five feet, six-inches across; and eight feet, nine inches deep. She weighed 187 tons.

The Captain of the Creole, Robert Ingram, was a Virginian, a career sailor, who made his living transporting slaves. He had been the master of the ship since it first sailed. Tall, thin, and strikingly handsome, he moved with an air of aristocracy about him. He loved sailing, and found that living at sea was preferable to ordinary land-based occupations. He disliked physical labor such as planting, and he refused to make his living in the service of others.

As the captain, he held absolute authority over the crew, the cargoes, and the vessel itself. Sometimes he thought he actually had power over the sea and tides. In fifteen years as a sailor and senior officer, no impediment had ever threatened his mastery over a vessel or its cargo. Sailors who served aboard his ships held a different opinion of the Captain. He never sailed at night, through a storm, or more than three hundred miles off the coast of the eastern seaboard.

"Fainthearted," some said. "Couldn't handle a dinghy," others remarked.

That he was a link in the evil flesh trade, fostering human misery, was not a consideration for forty-two year old Captain Ingram. He viewed the slaves as objects, much like cotton and tobacco. He commanded a ship, a lofty status that he believed was a natural consequence of his superior intelligence and indeed, his birthright. His cargo was in chains, his crew was mainly a band of bullies and drunkards, and his ship was half the size of a modern ocean-going vessel. None of this had much effect on Robert Ingram's sense of superiority. He was the Captain and that was all that mattered.

Zephemiah C. Gibson was employed as the first mate. He had lived at sea for thirteen-years, serving mostly on slave brigs. This was his second voyage aboard the Creole. Zephemiah was the twenty-eight year old son of a South Carolina minister who reared his children in the Puritan tradition. He left home at age fifteen and signed on to an English ship as a cabin boy. He loved the sea and the sailors who watched over him. He seldom stepped foot on land. Boyish in his appearance and demeanor, he was likeable and had no enemies at sea.

The Second Mate was Lucius Stevenson. He was a tall man, prematurely bald, and wore a red bandanna over his skull at all times. Two gold earrings dangled from each lobe, often glinting in the sun, drawing one's attention away from his scarred face and crooked nose. Lucius had a reputation for extreme cruelty to slaves when they were aboard ship. He had been previously dismissed from the

Congress for having thrown a slave overboard.

The Creole had begun its journey in early October 1841, sailing the James River out of Richmond, headed for the port of Hampton where she would put out to the open sea. Along the river they picked up slaves at different landings. In places where the Creole was unable to dock, they remained in the middle of the river. Sometimes a small boat came alongside, delivering one or two slaves.

Approaching Hampton, a half dozen male slaves rested in the dank darkness of the Creole's fore hold. Pompey Garrison, a bony, skeletal-faced, nineteen-year old slave sat with five other men on hard wooden benches, swatting away an occasional horsefly, or kicking at a bold and intrusive rat. They idled away their hours making small talk, occasionally stretching or napping on one of the several crude wooden bunk beds. Older men told Pompey that he talked too much and, jokingly, one man threatened to beat him into silence. Otherwise, they were docile and uncomplaining.

They were the first of the cargoes to be loaded aboard the Creole for shipment to New Orleans. They had come from farms and plantations throughout Virginia, their usefulness measured by their potential to bring a high price in Louisiana. Although they did not know each other before being placed in the hold, they bonded quickly as it was the nature of slaves to do. Their shared misery removed any need for formal introductions: They were African and they were slaves. Social niceties were an alien concept. They nodded or grunted their introductions, understanding immediately that they were one and the same, bound together in servitude, and destined to live in perpetual suffering. They were brothers, and they would be loyal to one another. Survival and heritage demanded it of them.

A thick-chested, dark-skinned man, about twenty-one years old, sat next to Pompey. He was bright-eyed and full of energy. "Where you come from?" Jourdon Phillips asked Pompey. "You so big-mouthed... like you know everything... you know where we headed?"

Pompey Garrison, quiet for once, opened one eye, squinting at his inquisitor. His dream of paradise would have to wait. He had a man who wanted to talk. "I come outta' Jackson, Mizzippee. We's going to Nawlens... get sold again. I bin there."

"New Orleans? You been there 'afore?"

Other men stirred at the news. "How far?" "How long a sail?" "What's it look like?" "Any pretty women?" They asked.

Pompey had an audience. He stood and faced them. "You boys ain't bin nowhere, has ya'? Why, I bin bought and sold three times already. ...made the run to Nawlens 'bout a year ago on the *Congress*. White man what bought me sold me to an Alabama lawyer."

"Why you coming out of Mississippi? ...how'd you end up here?" Jacob Haywood, a slim youth inquired.

Pompey realized that he was the only slave aboard with knowledge of how the slave trade worked, or at least how he believed it functioned. "Listen to me, boys.... I be maybe nineteen-years old and ain't chopped no cotton and I ain't never picked no okra. Neva! I just bin used for sellin'. The Alabama man sold me to a preacher soon as we got to Bu'minham. He were making a Colored boys' choir, he say. I stay there for a bit, then I up and run away—"

"You was free?" David Parker, another of the slaves asked. He stood up and faced Pompey. "You're telling a story."

"Ain't neva' told no lie, so help me."

"What happened? How'd you get away?"

Pompey grinned at his listeners. Although his body had been shackled, his creative mind was in excellent form. He had their full attention. "Ya'all ain't bin where I bin. Just listen real good to me. Time be comin' when we gets a chance and we all gets free. Now, 'bout that Alabama preacher... He come at me with a knife one dark night. Say he were gonna' make an 'alto' out o me. I don't know 'bout no alto, but I knew what he were fixin' to do with that knife. I run like a barnyard chicken with a hot-blooded rooster a chasin' it."

"Jesus, Lord" Jacob Haywood gasped.

"Yez'zuh, he were a fixin' to cut off my, ah... things. He say when he get done, I gonna' sing like an angel."

A rat scurried across the floor in front of them but no one took notice.

Jourdon Phillips eyed Pompey suspiciously. "Well you don't sound too screechy right now."

"I runs like a deer... almost made it to Tenn'see. Bounty hunters pick me up right quick... sell me to a Mizzippee' man up by Jackson. I come right back to Virginee. See, buyin' and sellin' is mostly the game now. It ain't 'bout no cotton."

Jacob Haywood, his eyes as round as saucers, kicked loose straw at Pompey's foot. You sure can tell a story, Brother. So what's next for you... for us?"

"We sits tight, Boys. They say the Savior be a comin'... gonna set us free."

"I wish," David Parker said."How do you know? When the savior be coming?"

"Any day now."

"What does he look like? I damn sure don't want to miss him," David Parker laughed."

"He black. He big as an ox."

"How you know all this?" Jourdon said.

"News travel fast on da' river. I knows."

"Stinks in here," David Parker said.

"It's the mule crap," Jacob Haywood offered. "Guess we better get used to it."

The group fell silent; listening to the waves beat a slow and steady rhythm against the hull of the ship.

Chapter Twenty-One

We Will Be Free

The command to move came quickly. Madison and the slaves silently stumbled down the hill overlooking Hampton harbor. They were herded into a large corral that usually held livestock. This day it held human cargo and Madison's group filed inside, joining other slaves from Virginia farms. The slaves within the enclosure, added to those aboard the ship, now numbered one-hundred and thirty-eight, including women and children.

Madison anticipated his impending revolution with relish. On the dock, he craned his neck, dodging his head back and forth, searching for Milinda, but the women were kept in separate corrals. The only evidence that she might be in these yards was the earlier comment by Andrew Bankhead: "I seen a gal like you say... had a small boy..."

On the morning of October 30, 1841, they were ordered onto the Creole. The women embarked first, the men standing in lines alongside the gangway. Madison watched each female trudge slowly up the walkway and onto the vessel, carrying their small children and baggage.

Somewhere near the rear of the line of stooped shouldered females, he spotted her.

"Milinda! Milinda!" he called out and she turned her head slightly. She then straightened her back and walked her child onto the deck.

"You damn fool," Andrew Bird said, jabbing Madison in the ribs. "Be still. You'll get us all whipped."

Madison was satisfied that Milinda had heard him. He longed to hold her in his arms. After the female slaves were loaded, the men were ordered aboard. Whips cracked and overseers cursed. Like robots, the chained men marched up the gangplank. Lucius Stevenson poked each slave with his whip as he counted them aboard.

Seaman on deck removed the shackles and directed the slaves to climb down a ladder into the fore hold. Madison was the last to enter, helping to shepherd the others below. He paused for several seconds at the bottom, adjusting his eyes to the dim light of oil lanterns. He made a quick visual search for Milinda and Isaac, but saw nothing. He could not call out—several guards had accompanied them into the hold. More lanterns were lit and Madison's eyes adapted to the improved lighting. He could hear the murmur of the women and the muffled squeals of children, but could not see them. A barrier of cotton and tobacco bales blocked his view. Madison eased between the cargo and stood in the shadows. His eyes scanned a group of nearly forty women. He searched for Milinda and Isaac among them. After several sweeps, he saw her. She was busy attending to Isaac and other children. His heart raced and he wanted to go to her, scoop her up in his arms and flee the ship. He decided instead to wait until the guards had either left or were sleeping, and then he would approach her. Madison found a spot among the other men, resting their backs against the wall of the ship. He listened to the loud demands of Lucius Stevenson as he laid down the rules for passage.

"You Niggras are not to mingle with the women. Do not come up on deck unless summoned. You get bread, pone, pork and coffee twice daily. You may come topside in small groups for air. Slop jars will be emptied regularly."

Satisfied that they had a cargo of passive and obedient slaves, the guards climbed the ladder to the deck, leaving Madison and his followers to their own designs. The hatch slammed shut and Madison sprang to his feet. Against the cautions of the other men, he moved quietly between the bales and into the women's section of the hold. Startled at his bold entrance, they stopped their chatter and stared at him. They had not seen a man in many days.

Milinda looked up and cried out: "Madison... oh, Madison. I knew it was you... you have come for me!" She raced to his open arms and they embraced as violently as that first night in his bed. The women smiled, some applauded, and another brought Isaac to him.

Madison hugged his boy and planted kisses on his forehead. "You've done well with him, Milinda. He is strong and handsome." He handed Isaac back to her, and then grew solemn.

"Listen to me Milinda, I am going to get you... all of us out of here. We will be free. Tell the women. I have a plan. Listen for the sound of revolution and I'll take you and Isaac far away from here. I promise."

He hugged Milinda again and instructed her to wait patiently for his signal. He turned and moved smoothly back to his position against the wall.

Chapter Twenty-Two

The Ship's Masters

In addition to the three officers aboard, the Creole had a crew of eight men to supervise the operation of the ship. There were six able seamen, a cook and the steward, William Gautier. He was a "free colored man," and as seafaring customs allowed, he was considered part of the crew. William, a man of some talent and a manipulative personality, had arrived in America on a Spanish sailing vessel. He had spent five years aboard the *Agua Sierra*, doing all that he could to endear himself to the Spanish captain. He served as a personal valet to the ship's master and other crewmen. He was a galley hand, an adequate cook, and had become bilingual; able to speak Spanish and English. He had mastered every service task that might keep him at sea. Unfortunately, in time, the captain grew tired of him and sold William to the owners of the Creole. By terms of the bill of sale, he was to be given his freedom five years hence. That time had passed and William now enjoyed the limited privileges of an emancipated Negro. He distained any notion of stepping upon American soil and had never done so. He was aware that his release papers, written in Spanish, would mean nothing to land-based bounty hunters. He had never been a 'cotton slave' and didn't intend to become one.

Priscilla, the captain's wife; their daughter Rosemary, and two nieces were on board. They looked forward to vacationing and a shopping spree in the city of New Orleans. The Ingram's owned a substantial dwelling in Richmond, but Priscilla seldom lived there. Married to a ship's captain, she had endured long periods of separation. Shortly after The Creole was commissioned she moved much of their possessions aboard the ship. "I can't bear to be away from you any longer, "she told Robert. "We'll go wherever you go, I do love you so."

In the salons' of Richmond, gossips had it that she distrusted Robert. "...has an appetite for young slave girls," they said. "Heard he fathered a 'high yellow'..."

Four other white passengers were on board: Theophilus McCargo, John R. Howard, William Henry Merkle, and Joseph Ligonier. Theophilus McCargo's father was principal owner of their slaves aboard, but did not travel with them. Theophilus believed his presence aboard the ship was necessary to ensure the safe arrival in New Orleans of his father's merchandise, and Thomas was glad to be rid of his son for a few weeks.

"You've produced an idiot," he once told his wife. "That boy couldn't organize a two-wagon funeral."

Since the elder McCargo thought Theophilus too inept to handle the responsibility; privately, the more experienced Mr. Howard had been placed in charge of all McCargo's slaves. Theophilus McCargo was part Scottish and part Irish. His heritage had endowed him with bright red hair and matching freckles across his cheeks and nose.

Overweight, only slightly educated, and even less logical in his day-to-day administrations on behalf of his father, he was every bit a buffoon. Even the slaves knew it.

John Howard was a Scot who immigrated to America in 1825. Within a year he had managed to secure a position with Thomas McCargo as an overseer. Tall and wiry, he was mean-spirited and slaves knew enough to stay out of his way. Thomas McCargo considered him an excellent manager, and insisted that John Howard accompany his cargoes.

William Merkle was a tough, pockmarked Virginian of twenty-nine and a long-standing seafaring man. He had most recently served as first mate on the slave brig *Orleans*. The ship was grounded for repairs at Hampton, and he agreed to take overall charge of the slaves aboard the Creole in exchange for his passage.

Joseph Ligonier was the assistant to the steward. At forty, he had long white hair, was stooped-shouldered, and spoke in whispers. His background was a mystery. Even-tempered and kindly, he seemed out of place aboard such a vessel as the Creole.

Thomas McCargo and William H. Goodfellow shared ownership of twenty-six of the slaves. McCargo owned another twenty-eight slaves outright. George Andrews and Herman Jones were partners in the slave-trading firm of Jones and Andrews. They owned twenty-three of the Creole slaves. New Orleans merchants Charlie Hackman and John Bogan owned eight of the Creole slaves and P. Rockford owned two females and a child. The Richmond slaver Edward Lockhart owned forty-one slaves. They had all paid heavy prices for shipment of their property and insisted on safety and strict rules aboard the Creole. In late 1841, owners were almost forced to use ocean transport despite its hazards. The price of a prime slave was approaching a thousand dollars each and increasing at regular intervals.

On the night of October 30, 1841, the Creole lay anchored at the port of Hampton. Captain Ingram looked down at the deck from the wheelhouse. All appeared quiet aboard his ship. He lit a pipe and sipped brandy from a silver goblet. "Fine weather... we sail at first light," he said to Zephemiah Gibson.

The following morning, the Creole rounded Cape Hatteras in calm seas. She sailed a course due south for the island of Abaco in the Bahamas. At noon on Sunday, November 7, 1841, her position was twenty-eight degrees, thirty-minutes north latitude and seventy-six degrees west longitude, or about two-hundred and seventy-five statute miles due east of present day Cape Canaveral. The ship was about one hundred and fifty miles north of the lighthouse at Marsh Harbor on Abaco Island in the Bahamas.

The vessel, badly overloaded, rocked to and fro, sickening several of the slaves below. The stench in the fore hold became unbearable until someone carried the slop topside and threw it overboard. Soon thereafter, seasick slaves were brought up for fresh air. Those below were forced to tolerate the disgusting odor.

At eight o'clock that evening, Captain Ingram stood at the rail and looked out upon the waters. As seafaring men are often able to do, he recognized his position without the aid of navigational instruments. The night, he observed, was pleasant and clear. The sky was bedecked with stars. Daylight would bring smooth sailing. "Heave to," Mr. Gibson," Captain Ingram ordered. "We'll anchor for the night."

First Mate Gibson eyed the Captain from his

position on the fore deck. "Aye, Sir!" Gibson repeated the order and a beehive of activity ensued. Men scurried into position like a well-rehearsed fire drill. Sails were lowered and the anchor dropped deep into the sea. The iron claws found purchase on the bottom and in a few minutes, the Creole was dead in the water.

Mr. Howard asked Gibson why they had stopped. "What's the delay? With this breeze, we could be in New Orleans in another day or two."

Gibson finished coiling a large rope and dropped it to the deck. "Mr. Howard, you have not sailed with us before. Captain always anchors here and waits for daylight. It'd be a disaster if we run aground on the rocks of Abaco."

"Well, it's a damn unnecessary delay. We have calm waters and generous winds." Howard stormed away.

Priscilla Ingram had made many trips to ports along the Atlantic. She was with her husband, they were living as a family, and she was on a perpetual vacation. She shopped and dined in the best establishments along the coast, never giving much attention to the cargoes Robert carried. After anchoring, she spoke to Rosemary and her teenage nieces, Angeline and Amanda: "Father has stopped for the night. Make ready for bed and say your prayers, now." She clapped her hands and smiled. The children immediately obeyed, donning cotton nightgowns, kneeling in prayer, and then crawling between clean white sheets. They lay their heads on soft pillowcases.

Below, hungry children of their own age lay on moldy straw or on their mother's laps, fending off rats, fleas, lice, and other vermin. They too, prayed before sleep came, but uttered little thanks for their blessings. They prayed for freedom.

Chapter Twenty-Three

The Mutiny

Most of the passengers and crew were asleep by nine o'clock. The women slaves and their children only dozed, restless, anticipating an unusual night. In the fore hold Madison Washington stood, brushing off hayseed and dust. He placed his hands on his hips and looked through the shadows at a collage of black faces. "Hey, Ya'all."

Richmond Butler, a strapping young man of twenty-three, rose first and faced Madison. Then he turned toward the others, beckoning to them with his eyes. Elijah Morris stood, and then Ben Johnson stood beside him. Pompey Garrison rose quickly and stood alongside George Gandy and America Woodis. One by one, men came to their feet, darting uneasy glances at one another. They stared at the black giant before them, waiting for his order.

"It is time," Madison said. "You know what each of you must do." He nodded to Elijah Morris.

Elijah scurried up the ladder, carefully opened the hatch and crept onto the deck. In a moment, against the darkness, he spotted First Mate Gibson and approached him from behind. Suh," he said, tapping Gibson on the shoulder, "I sorry to trouble you, but one of the men is with the women. Don't wanna' all get whipped 'cause of him."

Gibson was startled at the voice. He spun toward Elijah, digesting the implication of the message. He immediately called out, "Merkle, Billy Merkle! Come quickly, we've got trouble in the hold."

William Merkle, occupied on the quarterdeck, raced to join Gibson. "What's that you say... trouble?"

"Niggra here says one of the bucks is in with the women."

"We'll go down together," Merkle replied.

"I'll fetch a light. Damn dark in those holds... can't hardly see the bloody Blacks."

Gibson struck a match, lit a lantern and waited for Merkle to open the hatch. He took the eight steps into the hold, two at a time, intending to quickly resolve the issue and return topside. He was immediately seized and wrestled to the floor. A huge black hand covered his mouth.

Merkle began his descent, arriving just a few seconds after Gibson. Squinting about, he was startled to find Madison Washington standing behind him in the shadows. The other slaves were slumbering or otherwise quiet, resting against the hull or sitting stooped over on the benches.

Merkle asked Madison: "Are you the one who has been with the women? Did you break the ship's rules?" He pulled a short riding crop from his belt.

Madison replied, "Yes, it is I."

"You'll feel the consequence," Merkle said, and then raised the crop above his head, bringing it down hard towards Madison's face.

Madison grasped Merkle's whip, easily twisting it from his hands. "Never again will you raise a whip against me.... Never!" He pushed Merkle to the floor, and then climbed the ladder, making his way to the deck in three bounds.

Merkle, somewhat in shock, protested loudly. "You black son of a bitch! You'll be thrown overboard!"

Gibson squirmed free from his captors. "I'll do it myself," he yelled as he started up the ladder directly on the heels of Madison. They reached the deck at almost the same time.

Topside, Madison adjusted his eyes to the darkness, then turned, noticed Gibson, and shoved him to the deck. His powerful arms sensed little resistance. Madison knew he could kill him with one twist of his neck but was not ready for indiscriminate murder. Some might die, but he had other plans for the first mate.

Elijah Morris rose up out of the darkness, twisted a pistol from Gibson's hand as he drew it from beneath his shirt. Instinctively, he fired it at Gibson, knocking him back to his knees. Madison ducked, shouting, "No."

Elijah only grazed the back of Gibson's head. It was the first time he had ever fired a pistol. The first mate struggled to his feet and ran toward the cabins to alert the captain and the crew. Elijah followed close on his heels, waving the pistol.

Madison yelled into the hold, "Come on out, boys, we have commenced and must go through with it." Without pause, thirty-seven black men started up the ladder, one behind the other, pushing the man above him.

Gibson, holding the back of his head, pushed open the door of the captain's cabin. "I've been shot! The slaves have risen!" He shouted the same alarm as he raced down the deck.

Crew members stirred in their berths, asking each other if they had heard some commotion. A slave revolt was never far from their minds and they began to dress.

Captain Ingram did not immediately comprehend the seriousness of Gibson's message. "See to it... I'll be along in a moment."

Gibson ran back down the deck where the slaves were swarming out of the hold. They instantly pounced upon him.

"Let me have him," Peter Smallwood shouted, grabbing Gibson around the neck. A cry went up from the mutineers and they lunged at the first mate, striking him with sticks and clubs. One man slashed him across the chest with a large butcher knife. The knife wielding black man, crazed with emotion, swung his blade wildly. The other mutineers drew back instinctively, releasing Gibson. He ran to the rigging and climbed rapidly to the main top, a wooden platform about a third of the way from the top of the mast. Out of breath, he watched the mayhem unfolding below. He cowered on the small stand and remained silent.

Captain Ingram was stretched out on the floor of his cabin and was fully clothed when Gibson made his frenzied entrance. He had not joined his wife that night, as he intended to rise before dawn and be under way as soon as he could see. He rose slowly, rubbed the sleep from his eyes and decided it might be best to have members of the crew with him as he investigated the commotion. *I'll demand order, the sailors will force compliance, and I'll get a few more minutes of sleep before we sail.*

Captain Ingram carried his favorite bowie knife in his hand, believing that if he was armed, he might command more respect from the rebellious slaves. He walked rapidly to the forecastle and aroused the crew. "Arise, you men! Arise! There's a ruckus aboard. Execute your drills," he demanded. "Quell this disorder!"

Madison and a small group of mutineers surrounded the captain's cabin. They carried knives, handspikes, and clubs. Looking through the open skylight, someone threw water through the glass, extinguishing the cabin lanterns. A chorus rose from the slaves as the lights went out. "Kill them when they come out, kill the damn captain.... Kill the damn sons of bitches!"

Captain Ingram waited for more of his crew to assemble. He was confident that they would suppress the uprising. They had discussed the actions to be taken during any occasion of slave unrest aboard ship. As a reaction to the uprising on the *Amistad* two years before, every slave ship had a standard crew drill designed to quickly put a stop to any such disturbances.

Ben Johnson boldly approached the captain from behind and wrestled the bowie knife from Robert Ingram's hand, stabbing him with it several times. The captain and his few crewmen were too slow to react.

"Step back," Madison commanded, jumping between the captain and Ben. "We need the captain to steer the ship, don't kill him." He held off the others as the wounded captain withered in pain at his feet.

Captain Ingram heard Madison's words and struggled to his knees. He took the opportunity to crawl to the starboard side of the ship where he lay for a while, bleeding profusely. *Where is the damned crew? God, have they forgotten our drills*? Fearing that he might be pounced upon again, he found enough strength to pull himself up the rigging where he joined Gibson.

"Mr. Gibson, I am stabbed and I think I am dying," The captain gasped. He soon fainted from the loss of blood and Gibson lashed him to the mainmast to prevent his falling overboard. The vessel was now rolling heavily in the seas, partly from the waves, but mainly from the upheaval on board.

Gibson looked down at the chaos and heard someone cry out, "Kill the sons of bitches, kill every white person on board... don't spare anyone!" The blood thirst of the mutineers was evident. Thoroughly frightened, Gibson began to pray.

William Merkle, hearing the first pistol shot and the uproar that followed, pulled himself up from the floor of the hold. He extinguished his lantern and climbed to the deck. Horace Beverly, one of the mutineers, saw him surface from the hatch and immediately grabbed him from behind. He held Merkle by the shoulders while Marshall Pendelton, another slave, beat him on the head, neck and chest with a wooden club. Someone screamed from across the deck, "Kill him, kill him, by God!" Pendelton swung wildly, missed one blow and struck Beverly instead. Merkle twisted away by ducking low and spinning to his right. He ran to the crew's cabin. On the way he observed the captain making his way to the maintop. *Coward. I'll be the first witness against you at the inquiry.*

John Howard heard the cries of the mutineers and the wounded Gibson. He grabbed a musket from the stateroom of Lucius Stevenson, just as several hot-tempered slaves slammed open the door. Warner Smith and his brother, Alsey, and a half dozen other slaves faced Howard. "Now you fixin' to get it," Warner said. He and Alsey reached for Howard.

In a moment of sudden courage, John Howard approached them head on. He waved the musket back and forth, temporarily holding the small group at bay. "Get back, ye black sons-a-bitches!"

Phillip Jones, one of the blacks, threw a hand-spike at Howard and he reflexively fired the musket. The mutineers fell back in a cloud of smoke. No one was hurt and they soon realized it. The weapon had only been loaded with powder. Howard picked up the long pike and brandished it as if it were a musket.

"He got the musket. Watch out!" Pompey Garrison yelled.

In the darkness and confusion, the mutineers believed for a moment that the pike was a weapon of some sort and they fell back from the doorway. Howard stepped out onto the deck believing that he would gain the upper hand. He had been used to a life where Negroes obeyed his every word. He had never needed any help in making them cower before him.

"It's only a pike," Warner Butler, a skinny young man shouted. "Take him."

They rushed Howard, grabbed his arms and held him tightly. Ben Johnson stepped forward and sank the captain's bowie knife deep into his chest. Howard staggered back into the cabin and fell against a table, gasping, "My God, they have killed me." He then fell to the floor, bleeding and helpless.

The group dispersed, running about the cabins, searching for other officers or crew. Theophilus McCargo was hiding under a berth in his cabin. He had not come out to face the mutineers. He helped Howard to a berth and heard him say, "The damned Niggras has at last killed me." While Theophilus watched, unable or too inept to render aid, he held Howard's hand as he bled to death. Theophilus' life of privilege made him an unlikely candidate to take up the fight. He looked for a place to hide.

William Merkle slipped through the inky darkness, finally managing to reach the main cabin. He leaned
over and peered through the skylight. Seeing no movement, he started to enter through one of the open panes
but heard a scuffling noise behind him. He pulled back
and entered a separate vestibule sleeping area, the after
berths. He climbed onto a bed and covered himself with
bedclothes. Two female cabin slaves, having had somewhat
of a tolerable life aboard the Creole, instinctively sat on
the edge of the bed and tried to hide him. They had been
trained to serve the crew.

Blair Cummings, a sailor, was awakened by the
captain's cries. A large and aggressive man, he enjoyed a
good fight, having proved himself often in barroom scuffles
along the shipping lanes from Maine to Key Largo. "Get
up, you sorry jackals," he yelled to the crew. "We've got
a fight on board! Find a weapon and follow me."

Cummings was eager to join the melee. He
grabbed a handspike and raced onto the deck. He waded
into a small group of mutineers and managed to fell several
of them but was soon seized from behind and overpowered.
Elijah Morris took the handspike from him while others
grappled against his amazing strength. A sailor named
Antonio Romano swung a club and knocked down George
Portlock, one of the slaves grappling with Cummings.
Together, Cummings and Antonio retreated to the main
cabin, the rioters hot on their heels.

Lucius Stevenson cowered in that cabin. He had
been shaken by the captain's shouts and Howard's cry,
"I am shot." He tried to leave the cabin but met the rioters pursuing Cummings and Antonio. The mob cornered
Cummings, Romano, and Stevenson. George Gandy and
others pushed them all to the floor and attacked them,

pelting them with fists and kicking them.

Gandy shouted, "Your captain, your mate and Mr. Howard are dead and now we have you... you long tall son of a bitch. You will die tonight, Mr. Stevenson!"

The mutineers raged and threatened every white sailor or officer they came upon. Impulsively, the mob climbed over Blair Cummings and Lucius Stevenson and went in search of other crew members. "Where is Gibson?" they demanded to know.

Cummings and Stevenson seized their opportunity and got up. They ran to the first mate's stateroom and hid behind dressers and tall cabinets. The cries of crewmen begging for mercy echoed across the deck. "Be silent, don't move a muscle," Stevenson said. Stevenson held his breath and Cummings closed his eyes. The situation had gotten far out of hand and they both knew it. This was no isolated occasion of simple disobedience by a few slaves. This was a full-blown mutiny and they were powerless to stop it.

Madison led a band of seven or eight blacks to the door of Stevenson's stateroom. "This is his room, get him!" He kicked at the door as the others pushed against it.

"We have the musket... it is loaded," Madison shouted. "Come out and you will be spared. If you stay inside, we'll come in and get you."

Addison Tyler pointed the musket at the door. Stevenson opened the door and Addison spontaneously fired the weapon. Stevenson, expecting as much, deflected the musket away from him. He and Cummings made a break through the gaggle of insurgents. Amid the confusion of the musket shot and smoke, they managed to make it to the fore royal yard. Stevenson, although struck with a piece of wood and slashed at with a knife, climbed the ropes to a small platform where he begged openly for his life. No one climbed after him and he remained there.

Other slaves searched the starboard rooms. They soon discovered the captain's wife, daughter and nieces. Elijah Morris towered over Mrs. Ingram as she knelt, begging for her life and the lives of the children.

"Kill them," someone yelled.

Elijah Morris scowled at her for a moment, and then replied, "We won't harm you, but your damned husband and his mate we will have by God!"

Blair Cummings, in his dash for safety, was struck a severe blow on the head but he somehow managed to reach the open deck. Dazed, he started to climb the rigging when a slave, Richard Butler, shouted, "Who is that going up?"

Cummings gave his name and Richard demanded that he come back down or die in the rigging. A crowd gathered and Madison Washington called up to Cummings. "If you come down now, you will not be harmed. I give you my word."

Cummings concluded that this was the slave who led the insurrection. The ship was now his, and he was the master. Cummings meekly climbed down.

Madison and his followers passed the wheelhouse with Cummings. Several blacks advanced to kill him but Madison intervened, ordering them to spare the man's life. Ben Johnson protested. "We need to kill them all. If they don't have no witnesses, they ain't got no evidence."

Madison stopped his small band of mutineers, holding Cummings by the scuff of his neck. "There's been enough bloodshed. It was necessary, but we have the ship. No harm shall come to anyone else."

"Aw hell, Ben protested. Let's pay 'em back for

all the misery they gave us."

Cummings wiggled under Madison's big hand and he tightened his grip, almost lifting the sailor off the floor.

"Kill them all and we'll be adrift at sea," Madison said. "If they have no hope that they might live, why should they sail us to freedom?"

A slave known only as Dr. Ruffin replied. "We'll sail the ship to Africa ourselves. My heart will show us the way."

A cry of approval went up from the mutineers. "Hey, hey.... We'll go to Africa. Kill them!"

Madison threw Cummings to the deck where he cowered, afraid to move. "I feel the same as you," Madison said. He glared at the group confronting him. "I would like to kill them all, punish them as they have punished us, but that will only mean more suffering for our people. When word reaches shore, we will be condemned as heathen savages and our brothers and sisters will pay the price. There will be no more killing!"

Madison had made his point. No one opposed him further. The riot began to subside with only isolated pockets of activity scattered about the ship.

Chapter Twenty-Four

The New Masters

Benjamin Butler ordered one of the sailors to retrieve the bowsprit lantern which hung outside of the cabin to signal passing ships that the Creole was anchored there. Using the lantern, he, Madison, and America Woodis examined the remaining cabins.

Jacob Ligonier was cowering in a stateroom with Gautier, the steward; and Harriet Lewis, a female McCargo slave. Harriet had been a steward's assistant during the voyage. "What do you want with me?" Ligonier asked.

"Your skin and that of the steward, too," Elijah Morris threatened.

"Throw them in the hold," Madison ordered.

Before Ligonier reached the deck he heard someone shout, "Kill every God damn white person on board and if no one will, I will!" He concluded that whoever spoke, it must be the ringleader and would commit murder that night if he had not already done so.

Theophilus McCargo remained hidden behind the furniture in his stateroom during the fight. He watched as the slaves entered the cabin areas. He could identify Ben Johnson, Elijah Morris, Madison Washington, and another man they called Jim. *That's Jim Jones, one of my father's slaves.*

The search party soon noticed that the tall dresser looked out of place; too far out from the wall.. The rioters reached out for him and McCargo shouted. "Jim, are you going to kill me? I always treated you well."

"Is that you, Theophilus?"

"Yes.... Please, I beg of you... don't kill me," McCargo whimpered.

Jim turned to the others: "Boy's don't hurt him. He ain't worth the time."

Madison ordered that McCargo be taken to the hold and thrown in with the rest of the prisoners.

Seeing Howard's body in the berth, Morris and Johnson ordered that it be taken up on deck. "Get that white devil out of here," Morris said. "Cut off his head and feed him to the sharks!"

Mr. Merkle remained concealed under the bedclothes. He heard voices calling out, "Where is Merkle, bring him out! He shall not live by God!" The two black women who had been protecting Merkle became frightened and scurried through the door. No one stopped them. Merkle, terrified, crawled deeper under his mattress but was soon discovered and dragged out. Ben Johnson and Elijah Morris waved their knives and poked at him as he danced and parried their halfhearted thrusts.

"I am a navigator," Merkle pleaded. "I can take you to any port. Please spare my life and I will guide this ship for you."

Madison considered Merkle's pleas. "Leave him alone, I want to talk to this prisoner."

The others quieted and allowed Madison to speak with Merkle. "I want you to sail this ship to Liberia," Madison told him. "Do it and you might live to tell your children."

"There are not enough provisions... water for a journey of that length," Merkle informed him. "We would die at sea from thirst or starvation."

Dr. Ruffin chimed in, "We should head for one of the British islands, they're closer."

"He's right," Ben Johnson agreed. "I hear that many a slave been set free by the Johnny Bulls. Them that gets shipwrecked on the islands is free to go."

"You are sure?" Madison asked.

"Last year the *Harmosa* shipwrecked off Abaco." Ben explained. "The slaves were taken to Nassau by a English ship. Their queen freed them."

Madison spoke. "Then we go to Nassau." He looked at William Merkle, ashen with fear. "We will spare Mr. Merkle's life in return for his navigating this ship to the British port and the queen of the English."

Ben Johnson found William Gautier and grabbed him by the shirt. "Where's the damn liquor?"

Gautier rummaged through the captain's cupboards and produced four bottles of brandy, a jug of whiskey, and a demijohn of Madeira. Elijah, Jim, Ben, and several others quickly consumed most of it, and then called for bread and apples, which Gautier hastily supplied.

Ben grew somewhat intoxicated from the liquor. He sat on the edge of the captain's bed with the blood covered bowie knife in his hands. He bragged, "I done sent many of them to hell this night."

Madison led a search of the deck looking for the captain and the rest of the crew. At about four thirty in the morning, Elijah spotted Gibson in the maintop. "Madison, look up... it's the first mate!"

A group of mutineers gathered at the foot of the main mast. "There's someone with him," a man shouted.

"Come down, Mr. Gibson," Madison ordered.

Gibson shook with fear. He had witnessed four of the insurrectionists bringing Howard's body onto the deck and throwing him overboard. He looked anxiously at the cluster of men gathered below and feared that he too, would soon taste the salt of the sea. Gibson remained silent.

"If you do not come down we will shoot you down," Madison shouted.

Gibson sighed and summoned his courage. He had little choice and he hastily clambered down. "What will happen to me?" Gibson asked Madison when his feet hit the deck.

"You will assist Mr. Merkle in landing this ship on a British island or you will be thrown overboard."

Ben Johnson joined Madison and the others. He carried the musket in one hand, a liquor bottle in the other. He thrust the muzzle of the musket against Gibson's chest. "And you'll be headless, too. What do you say?"

Gibson stammered, "Whatever you wish."

"Who is that in the maintop?" Madison asked.

"The captain."

Ben Johnson ordered the unconscious Captain Ingram to come down. When he didn't answer, Gibson said, "The captain is too weak from the loss of blood. He cannot climb down."

Simultaneously, Elijah Morris, Harry Brown and others discovered Lucius Stevenson in the fore royal yard and they ordered him to come down. "You damn son of a bitch, come down and receive your due," Elijah said.

Stevenson gingerly picked his way down, but at the halfway point he stopped, afraid to descend any farther. "Are you going to kill me?

"Come down and find out," Elijah said.

Stevenson climbed the remainder of the way down and landed on the deck. "Please," he begged, just give me a few minutes to talk with you. I can help..." He promised to bring them to an English port if they would not kill him.

Gibson's voice echoed from the poop deck and Stevenson asked if he could go to the first mate, believing that Gibson was negotiating with the mutineers and he might include himself in any bargain they struck. Dr. Ruffin and Elijah Morris escorted Stevenson to Gibson. "I can use him to help me navigate," Gibson said. "Spare his life... let him resume his duties."

Madison did not trust Stevenson, having observed his regular abuse of slaves, his cowardice, and his manipulations in getting to speak with Gibson. "Take a bottle of water to the captain in the maintop before he falls into the sea."

Stevenson climbed to the top, stopping beside the wounded captain. He shouted down that Captain Ingram was near death. Madison looked around and collared another sailor. "Take a rope to the top and help Stevenson make a sling. Bring the captain down."

In due course, Captain Ingram and Stevenson were on the deck. "Lock them in the fore hold and place a guard on them," Madison commanded.

The sun rose as a fiery red ball across the horizon. It served to signal that the mutiny was over and a new day was at hand... a new master commanded this ship. Madison ordered the crew to assemble on deck. He demanded that they set sail for a Caribbean island, "Any island so long as the Queen lives there."

Several crew members laughed at Madison's reference to Queen Victoria's place of residence. It irked him. "Set sail now or swim to shore!" He thundered.

The laughter died out quickly. "Aye, Aye, Sir!" someone called out.

"We're going to Africa," a man shouted.

"They'll shipwrecked us," a sailor complained.

Another sailor called out. "You want to go to Freeport... Nassau... in the Bahamas. It is a British territory. Queen Victoria does indeed reside there."

"Let Gibson and Merkle steer the ship," Madison said. "But keep a close eye on them."

The sailors huddled together and waited for instructions. "Make passage to Freeport," Madison told them. "Now!"

The sailors scurried about to do Madison's bidding. The sails were set, the anchor raised, and the Creole got under way, bound for Nassau. It was fully daylight, the night having raced past them.

Not all of the slaves had taken part in the revolt. Many of them were afraid, having spent countless years in submissive service to their white masters. When Madison was told of the reluctance of some slaves to assist in the operation of the ship, he climbed down into the after hold. As if by magic, when his feet appeared on the ladder, the unwilling slaves gathered in a semicircle. The women flooded into the small space from the fore hold, coming out from behind the bales and boxes of cargo.

Milinda eased her way to the front, holding Isaac's hand. When all of the slaves were present, Madison paused a long while, looking at each of them, scrutinizing their faces for evidence of agreement or disagreement for what he had done. He planted his hands on his hips and looked at Milinda and Isaac, then at the crowd.

"You are on your way to freedom," he said. "You may not have chosen to be a part of this rebellion, but it is God's will. Unless you help in the deliverance of this ship to Nassau, I will throw overboard any person who defies my orders."

"We don't know what to do," a young orphan boy wept. "I'm afraid."

"You have nothing to fear now, Albert Henning," Madison replied. "It is over. We are the masters of this ship and the masters of our future. You are free. You will never hear the crack of a whip again or carry a load that you do not wish to carry."

The audience stirred with the news; their fears subsided. "Amen," someone shouted. "Praise God," said another. They began to murmur, and then sing softly.

Madison waved his hands for silence. "I, and the other men who have defied the white devils are prepared to give our lives for your freedom. In a few days, you will be under the good queen of England's protection."

"What can we do to help?" Rheuben Foster asked in a strong voice. "I am ready..."

"You able-bodied men get upstairs and lend your labors to the sailing of this ship."

Men jumped to obey him and a scramble of bodies started up the ladder. Milinda watched her husband. She said nothing, but her face beamed with pride for her man. He was keeping his promise to her and she would keep her promise to him. She would love him forever.

The women and children followed the men onto the deck. They would not return to the hold below except to gather necessities and baggage. Madison ordered that the captain be taken to Milinda, where she could treat his injuries. Soon, all of the ship's wounded were lining up to have their cuts and abrasions treated by their black masters. Slave women, from years of necessity, were skilled at improvised medical remedies, treating childhood illnesses, tending to the sores and injuries of field hands and delivering their own babies.

Later that day Madison allowed Stevenson to come on deck and help Gibson take an observation to determine their position. The object of much suspicion, Ben Johnson ordered Stevenson back to the hold after he argued with Gibson about their location on the sea. "You'd better stay below," Ben told Stevenson. "There are many men who'd like to throw you overboard."

Elijah Morris watched the discussion between Stevenson and Johnson. He approached the hatch where Stevenson was imprisoned. "Stevenson," Morris called out. "I do not want to see you hurt but they talk of throwing you overboard tonight... after they cut your head off."

Lucius Stevenson quivered at the news. "Please inform your leader, Mr. Washington. Ask him to spare my life."

"I don't know that anybody can help you, Mate," Elijah said. Then he sought out Madison and told him about Stevenson cowering in the hold.

"The ship needs all hands," Madison said. "Bring the second mate back up, but keep an eye on him." When the shaking Stevenson arrived on deck for the second time, Madison told him to resume his duties with Gibson.

Sometime after nine o'clock, while Stevenson walked the deck alone, he heard a shot and felt the whistle of a lead ball passing by his head. He immediately hit the deck and covered his head with his hands. "God help me," he whispered.

Gibson heard the shot and came out of the wheel-house. "Go aloft, Mr. Stevenson. You'll be safer there. See if you can see the lighthouse at Abaco."

Stevenson climbed the rigging, stopped halfway up and looked below him. He saw Ben Johnson reloading the pistol. He clambered higher, hoping to get out of range. Ben and another former slave laughed at Stevenson's haste in getting to the top. During the next few hours, Ben periodically left the deck, hiding from Stevenson's view. He raced back to the bottom of the rigging when he thought Stevenson might attempt to climb down. After several episodes of these cat and mouse antics, Ben tired of the sport and left. Stevenson climbed down and faced Madison at the bottom.

"I spoke to Ben. Go about your duties, Mr. Stevenson. You won't be bothered again."

The men participating in the mutiny separated themselves from those who did not. Their daring accomplishment automatically made them superior to the others, they believed. Dr. Ruffin remarked that there was nothing like success in battle, "I feel good!"

The mutineers stationed themselves about the ship to watch for any attempts by the crew to retake the vessel. Guards were placed to watch the prisoners in the fore and after holds. All of the slaves were now on deck breathing, "free fresh air," as Madison described it. Milinda joined him for a while, but out of concern for Isaac, he told her to remain with the women. "We will be together soon enough," he said. They embraced and parted.

Madison, Dr. Ruffin, Ben Johnson, and Elijah Morris took turns watching the officers. Dr. Ruffin and

George Portlock knew the letters of the compass and Pompey Garrison told Madison that he had traveled to New Orleans before and knew the way. "Ah kin spot the landmarks if'n we come at that coast," he said.

Madison and the others established their headquarters in the captain's cabin. Ben Johnson sat at Captain Ingram's desk, swiveling in his chair. He asked Elijah Morris, "did you really plan on killing all the whites?"

No," Elijah replied. "We'll have to let them go when we dock at Nassau."

Ben Nodded, "If we have too much blood on our hands, the queen could turn against us."

"Might hafta' kill her too," Elijah said. "After I use her up."

They laughed. Ben handed Elijah the last of the rum and he rolled two cigarettes from tobacco he had taken from a sailor. He handed one to Elijah, then lit his own. Blowing out a long stream of smoke, he remarked, "Damn, it's all good."

Chapter Twenty-Five

Nassau

On Tuesday, November 9, the second day after the revolt, Madison watched a small pilot boat approach them from the port side. They were about a mile out from the Nassau lighthouse, which they could see. The pilot and his three crewmen were blacks, Freeport sailors from Nassau. They climbed rope ladders to board the ship. The pilot and his men immediately intermingled with the passengers, learning of the mutiny. "In Nassau, you'll be free... able to do as you please," the pilot said.

The Creole entered Nassau harbor at about eight o'clock in the morning. Slowly it maneuvered alongside a pier, jutting some two hundred feet out from the shore. Under the watchful eyes of Dr. Ruffin and Elijah Morris, crewmen tied the Creole to the dock.

The quarantine officer came alongside and as he did so, Gibson jumped into his boat. The surprised official stared at him. "There has been a damned mutiny on board," Gibson said. "They killed a man. Take me to the authorities!"

The quarantine officer took Gibson to the residence of the American Consul, John Bascombe, and then returned to watch the ship as it rested alongside the pier.

Consul Bascombe, a pudgy middle-aged man, had been the American representative in Nassau for little more than a year. He had failed to make many friends among the islands' civil servants, frequently showing his disdain for anything or anyone British.

Gibson was ushered into Consul Bascombe's office where he explained the events aboard the Creole during the previous two days. Together they raced to the Government house and asked to see the British Governor General of the Bahamas, Sir Francis Cochoran.

"Why are you so breathlessness, Gentlemen?" Governor Cochoran asked.

Gibson related the details of the mutiny to Sir Francis, and then Consul Bascombe demanded: "You must take steps to prevent the slaves from escaping and arrest these damned murderers."

Governor Cochoran, an elderly man with almost fifty years of government service, leaned back in his chair. He had served the Crown during the War of 1812, and had helped forge the Treaty of Ghent in 1815. Sir Francis despised Americans.

"Sir, may I inform you of a few matters of which you may not be aware, or perhaps you refuse to accept. The people you refer to as slaves are not slaves in Nassau. They are passengers aboard your ship. Whilst you are guests of Her Majesty, you will treat them with all the dignity she expects of one human being to another. Understood?"

Consul Bascombe and Gibson were speechless. Bascombe's face turned red and Gibson stammered: "Passengers?"

"Furthermore, Consul," Sir Francis continued. "I do not believe I have the authority to arrest anyone solely on your report. Perhaps they were defending themselves against your notorious American brutality."

Consul Bascombe interrupted: "Sir, I fully understand British law as it applies to visitors to your shores, however, we do have agreements regarding lawlessness... murder, to be more specific."

Sir Francis stood up. "What would you have me do...? Our laws are clear. Your passengers are no longer slaves. We have no extradition treaties."

"You won't help us?" Gibson asked.

"Well... I suppose I must do something, but I'm not inclined to assist you independently. I am obliged to consult with our Attorney General before I take any action. You'll have to wait until I hear from him."

"My government will be outraged," Consul Bascombe seethed.

"We've outraged each other before, Consul. We can tolerate it again for the sake of humanity." Sir Francis instructed Gibson and Bascombe to write a statement describing the mutiny and to make an official appeal for assistance.

"I'll confer with our Attorney General and inform you of his opinion." Sir Francis turned his back to the two men, dismissing them.

A note was dispatched to the Nassau Attorney General, George Andrews, and within a few hours, Sir Francis had his reply. It read: "In the matter of the passengers aboard the American vessel Creole, I well know from conversations with the governor, and from the many opinions of officers of the government, and that of private individuals, which I have frequently heard expressed, that it would be deemed a violation of the laws of Great Britain, in any manner, to molest or prevent slaves from obtaining their freedom, if once within the jurisdiction of the colony, no matter in what manner they might arrive or be brought within their jurisdiction, and therefore that a request in writing to forward the Brig Creole on to her destination with the residue of the passengers on board would be deemed unlawful under British law.

"I am aware that several of the passengers have been accused of a crime: not on a British vessel, upon British waters or on British territory. Treaties with the Government of America should be treated with all respect and consideration; therefore, an investigation of the circumstances concerning the events aboard the Creole should commence. It is highly advisable to restrain the accused passengers, but to release all others to the protection of The Queen."

Signed/

George C. Andrews

Attorney General

Sir Francis studied the opinion of the Attorney General for a few minutes, and then called for his secretary. "Take a message to the captain of the garrison."

Consul Bascombe decided to board the Creole and appraise matters for himself. At the dock, he received a note from Sir Francis informing him that a British military party would board the ship and take custody of it. Bascombe hurried to the vessel, boarding ahead of the military guard. He found the ship all quiet with only a few passengers lounging about. A doctor had accompanied him and he went to work examining the wounded. "Fine job those women did," the doctor commented as he examined several cuts and abrasions. "Spider web... amazing. I have little to do here."

The military guard arrived. It consisted of twenty privates, a corporal and a sergeant, under the command of a lieutenant. Their two longboats idled alongside the ship while the soldiers clambered up the ladders. All of the guards were black with the exception of the white officer, Lieutenant Manson.

Members of the crew surrounded Lieutenant Manson as soon as he arrived on deck. "I am in charge of this ship and all of her passengers," he announced. His men scurried about, running at port arms, securing all sections of the vessel.

Excellent, Lieutenant," Consul Bascombe said. "Round up the mutineers, the killers."

After a short discussion with the seamen, they identified and arrested Madison Washington, Elijah Morris, Dr. Ruffin and Ben Johnson. They were bound at the wrists and placed in the brig's longboat.

"They should be flogged, immediately," Consul Bascombe said.

Lieutenant Manson faced the Consul. "Sir, with utmost respect, I must advise you that I am in charge, not you. There will be no mistreatment of these prisoners." Lieutenant Manson issued instructions that the detainees be given food and water. He then commenced an investigation, speaking to all crew members and some passengers. His investigation was methodical and time consuming, and the prisoners were left in the longboat with little to do. They fell into conversation periodically, each of them attesting that they had no regrets for what they had done.

"Milinda and Isaac will know freedom," Madison said. "That's all that matters to me. I may hang, but they will be as free as the African lion."

"If just one of us gets to freedom, "Dr. Ruffin said, "it was all worth it. I've lived long enough."

"I always thought I'd die at the end of a rope anyway," Ben Johnson said.

Elijah Morris agreed with the others. "If I do get free, I damn sure ain't coming back to find me no woman. ...you hear what I say, Madison?"

They spent their time watching the goings-on aboard the vessel, dozing and then conversing when the notion hit them. The tropical sun beat upon them, making them uncomfortable, but no one complained. Madison remarked that it appeared they would be in the boat for a long time; Lieutenant Manson was so meticulous. In the late afternoon he asked a guard if their hands might be unbound so that they could relieve themselves.

"Piss in your pantaloons," the corporal said.

"It ain't pissin' I got to do," Elijah replied.

Lieutenant Manson was summoned. He relented and allowed their hands to be untied. He ordered that a tin kettle be brought to the long boat as a convenience for toilet matters.

Ben Johnson remarked, "That pisspot ain't big enough for what I'm fixin' to do." He laughed heartily.

"Pisspot gotta' have a name," Dr. Ruffin said. Her name gonna' be 'Tilley.'"

"Where'd you come up with that?" Elijah said.

"First girl I knew... name was Tilley. I pissed—"

"My God," Madison said. "Here we are, incarcerated, and perhaps headed to the gallows, and you boys are talking nonsense."

Dr. Ruffin studied Madison for a bit. Although he was only three years older than the leader of the revolt, he had had a lifetime of harsh conditions and was well beyond his years in experience. He was as perceptive and sly as any older man might be. "Incarcerated...? Perhaps...? You talk like you're white, Washington. You had book learnin'?"

"In a way," Madison said. "I had a gifted teacher when I lived on the King plantation. When I was free, up in Canada, my white family schooled me a bit. Mister Smith, the trail rider that brought me to Richmond... he told me all about the world."

"What'd he tell you?" Elijah asked.

"He told me about Liberia, England, and Jamaica... free places. He told me about the war that's coming."

"Freedom war?" Ben Johnson asked. "Too bad we won't live to see it."

Madison looked over the most important men in his life at that moment. He realized that by virtue of his having planned the mutiny, he had naturally become responsible for this bloody act of defiance. He decided to share his thoughts with them. They had had the courage to stick with him, to put their lives in jeopardy. They deserved to know all that he knew.

"I was lucky," Madison said. He smiled, wiped his forehead with a kerchief, and began. "I was brought up as a favored slave of a decent white woman. She hired a teacher for me and I learned to read from the bible. Most of what I know comes from the good book."

"Uh huh," Elisah said. "Ain't a bad place to start." He shifted his back against one of the seats of the long boat, knowing he'd be listening to Madison for a while.

Madison continued. "When God made the world, He put the first man in Africa... a black man. That's where we come from. He told him and his wife not to eat from a tree in His garden—"

"Preacher," Dr. Ruffin said. "You quotin' Gospel. Now, how the hell did we get from that garden to here?"

"Not preaching, just the truth." Madison said. "The way I see it, this miserable situation began right about the time God told Adam and Eve not to eat that forbidden fruit."

"What was it," Ben asked. "An apple like they say? If it was in Africa, I 'spect it was a cocoanut."

"Not a real fruit, Ben," Madison said. "It's just a way of saying that they got knowledge... they came to learn about evil; something they didn't know about before. It pulled them left and right. Not long after, their children started killing each other. Cain killed his brother Abel, because he was jealous about what he had. People have been trying to rule over each other ever since."

"Right now, they wanna' kill us. Why white folks so ornery?" Dr. Ruffin asked.

"Yes, they are, but not all of them. Anyway, that's not so important," Madison said. He shifted his position, leaned back and put his arms behind his head. He was enjoying the role of teacher.

"Don't matter?" Elisah retorted. "Matters to me."

"I mean that there is a larger story... you heard about the flood?"

Dr. Ruffin sat up. He had some ability to read and like Madison, had been schooled in bible stories. "You talkin' about Noah and them animals that went up the plank, two by two?"

"That's it, Dr. Ruffin. They were all African; my teacher told me so."

"Hold on, Preacher," Elisah said. "If we was all

African, how'd they get white and we's still black?"

"I asked Miss Agnes about that. She believed it was from what they ate and where they lived. She said the fish-eaters crossed the waters and went north looking for food. The sun and the winter and what they ate turned them white. I guess our ancestors just stayed where Noah put us off." Madison laughed.

"This Miss Agnes, she black or white?" Dr. Ruffin asked.

"She was African, like us. She ate pork and she hated fish.... drank rum."

The men roared with laughter and clapped their hands. "Madison be a storyteller for sure," Elijah said.

One of the cabin girls came by and delivered them a supper of boiled potatoes, greens, and baked fish.

"We's gonna' turn white," Dr. Ruffin said.

No one returned to tie their hands.

Chapter Twenty-Six

The Soul Of A Slave

Consul Bascombe's sympathies for the American crew members and other white persons aboard became obvious soon after he boarded. He told Lieutenant Manson that no "colored persons" were to leave the ship, but that the whites would be free to come and go as they pleased. "That comes directly from Sir Francis," he lied.

Lieutenant Manson shot him a piercing glance. "If you say so... Yes, Sir."

Consul Bascombe returned to dockside with the injured Captain Ingram and two other wounded crewmen. At the dock, he was handed a message from the Governor General, requesting him to attend a session of the islands Governing Council. "They are discussing the situation as regards the American brig Creole," the note read.

Consul Bascombe raced to the Government house where Sir Francis, seated behind his huge desk, read to him the results of the Council's deliberations. Bascombe had missed the meeting and his opportunity to speak on behalf of United States interests.

"You are quite late, Sir... but this is the immediate decision of the council," Sir Francis said. He adjusted his spectacles and read aloud: "One: That the courts of law in the Nassau colony has no jurisdiction over the alleged offenses. Two: That since a charge of murder has been formally lodged, an investigation should take place in order that the alleged guilty parties not be allowed to go about at large. At the conclusion of the investigation it will be decided whether to hand the alleged guilty persons over to the American government or not, or to be otherwise disposed of. Three: That as soon as the investigation is complete, all persons aboard the Creole, not implicated in the alleged offenses, must be released from further restraint. And four: a detailed account of what has transpired will be transmitted to the British Minister in Washington."

Sir Francis placed the memorandum on his desk and removed his spectacles. "Does the notion that some of your 'Cargoes' might be set free trouble you, Consul?"

"On the contrary, I'm pleased that an investigation will take place. I insist on being a part of it."

"This is a British inquiry, but very well, I suppose you do have interests..."

"My superiors would judge me negligent if I did not protect American rights and property."

Sir Francis sighed, but gave him permission to secure the services of Robert Duncan, the police magistrate; and John Burnham, Justice of the Peace of the colony. These two middle-aged white men had only modest experience in police investigative work, the island having very little criminal activity. They commandeered a small boat and paddled their way out to The Creole. Able seaman helped them aboard. They proceeded to examine witnesses all day and into the evening with special interest in Madison and the ringleaders. John Burnham insisted that Madison and his friends be removed from the longboat and placed in the hold. "These men are suffering in this heat, give them water and allow them to move about,' he said.

"Humbug," Consul Bascombe remarked, but did not interfere.

Lieutenant Manson directed several guards to comply with the order. Madison led the small group across the deck toward the hatches. A modest applause erupted from the former slaves, now lounging about the deck, chatting and developing possible answers for their own interrogations.

The next day, November 10, the examinations continued. The inquisitors determined that although approximately thirty-seven slaves had participated in the mutiny, only nineteen could be positively identified.

John Burnham took several members of the crew aside and questioned them. Joseph Ligonier, having overheard the excited comments of the mutineers, insisted he knew who killed Mr. Howard.

"Be specific" Mr. Burnham ordered. "Thus far, I've had nothing but conflicting testimony."

"Indeed. A mutiny is a confusing thing," Ligonier replied. "Especially in the dark. But in the cabin, when they wanted whiskey, I heard them all talking. Ben Johnson said he did it."

"He said as much?" Burnham asked as he jotted notes on a pad. "Exactly what did he say?"

Ligonier stammered. "Well, ah... He said he had sent a lot of them to their graves this night."

William Gautier, the black steward, interrupted. "Sir, Mr. Ligonier wasn't in the cabin when that statement was made. He was on the deck. I mentioned it to him later."

"Well then, that's only hearsay." John Burnham said. "Besides, it sounds like a boast. Only Howard was killed, not "many of them." What else, Mr. Ligonier?"

Ligonier paused. "I suppose it could have been Morris, he did a lot of bragging'."

Burnham studied Ligonier. "Damn it, Man. You cannot name the assassin with any certainty. If Morris or Johnson did it, what about this fellow, Washington, and the man they call Dr. Ruffin. What did they do?"

"Ruffin shot his mouth off, too. Claimed he killed several of our sailors."

"And Washington?"

"He's the ringleader, everybody will agree on that. I know he had a hand in the killing'."

John Burnham frowned. "You are free to go, gentlemen."

Dr. Ruffin was taken from the hold to a cabin for questioning by the magistrate, Robert Duncan. He said very little during his grilling. He refused to implicate any of the others in the plot and denied knowing anything about Mr. Howard's death.

"You may be charged with murder, Mr. Ruffin. I remind you, we have credible witnesses."

"Hell, if you has these cat-eyed witnesses, then you don't need me."

"It was Washington, that big Black, wasn't it?"

Dr. Ruffin thought about that remark for a moment. "No, it was not Madison Washington. It was me what done it."

"You killed Mr. Howard! I hardly believe you. You are protecting Washington."

Dr. Ruffin refused to speak further. Ben Johnson was interrogated next.

Duncan shook a finger at Ben. "You thrust the knife into Mr. Howard's chest and killed him. Dr. Ruffin told us as much."

"The hell he did."

"Come with me," Duncan ordered. He marched Ben into the same cabin where Howard had died, pointing at a pool of dried blood. "This is where the dastardly deed was done.

"If you say so. But you're just fishin'."

"You'll hang, Ben Johnson."

Ben had thrown himself vigorously into the mutiny, and indeed, he had been the first to stab Mr. Howard. He was certain that Dr. Ruffin had not pointed him out. He was noncommittal and said little more, except that he had not killed Mr. Howard.

"If you didn't kill him, then who was it... that black bastard, Washington?"

Ben studied the police magistrate. "I change my mind. It was not Madison. I stabbed the son of a bitch and I'm glad of it."

Duncan closed his notes and looked at John Burnham. "Now we have two admitted assassins."

Elisah Morris was hardly questioned; the interrogators having grown weary of the fruitless investigation. Elisah likewise insisted that he alone killed Mr. Howard. The investigating committee, with the assistance of Lieutenant Manson and his guard, decided to question and record the depositions of everyone on board. Lieutenant Manson lined up every former slave on the deck. As he and his men went through their ranks, they asked but one question: "Who killed Mr. Howard?"

Every adult slave, looked Lieutenant Manson in the eye and responded, "It was I, Sir."

Madison was the last to be interrogated. He was obviously the most important member of the mutiny, the person most likely to have committed the murder and Magistrate Duncan wanted the glory of obtaining his confession. Alone in a stateroom with Madison, Duncan adopted a casual and friendly attitude toward him. He invited Madison to sit and then sat opposite him.

"Mr. Washington," he began. "Be assured that my query is purely one of personal interests, not intended to result in charges against you. Now I understand the plight of slaves and certainly sympathize with you. Why, if I were a Colored... in your shoes, I might have done the same."

Madison nodded. He understood the ruse perfectly: He was to believe that anything he might say was of no consequence, and then they would use his own words to hang him.

Duncan continued. "Here in Nassau, the means by which you arrived are not important; consequently, anything you say about the mutiny will not be held against you. It took place at sea... we have no jurisdiction."

"Yaz Suh."

"In fact, I rather admire your spirit. Now why don't you just be at ease and tell me all about it... on an informal basis of course. Describe the events. Who might have killed Mr. Howard?"

Consul Bascombe and John Burnham waited outside the cabin door listening for Madison's reply.

"He's the instigator," Bascombe whispered. "We don't need any evidence... just hang the bastard."

"Suh, I don't know 'bout no killin'. 'It were pitch dark.... I didn't see nothin'," Madison stammered.

"Come now, Mr. Washington, you can do better than that. My impression of you is that you are an educated man, well spoken, and quite capable of arousing others to follow you. They say you planned and led the revolt. Do you intend to sit there and pretend that you know nothing of the events; that you saw nothing... you were not a part of it?"

"Yaz Suh."

Duncan, exasperated and insulted at Madison's feigned ignorance, exploded. "Tell me, you black son of a bitch! Who killed Mr. Howard? Who were the participants in the mutiny? So help me, you'll hang in Jackson Square, regardless."

Madison showed no fear. "As you wish, Magistrate. I did all that you say, all that you accuse me of."

"You planned and led the revolt?"

"Yes."

"You stabbed and killed Mr. Howard?"

"That too."

"I'm surprised at you, Mr. Washington. You are willing to take all the blame? Then you alone will hang for it. Come now, what role did the others play?"

"They are innocent.... I put the knife into Mr. Howard's belly."

Consul Bascombe and John Burnham burst into the room. Bascombe stood before Madison, shaking with rage. "I knew it was you, you damned heathen. I'll celebrate your death."

"And now, just what have you to say for yourself?" John Burnham asked. "We'll be taking our report to the Governor. Your trial and subsequent hanging shall be quickly forthcoming, I am certain."

Madison stood and faced his inquisitors. "Anything to say? Grant me the time... It was not done on impulse, you may be sure."

"I am keenly interested in what motivated you to kill another human being, Mr. Washington," Duncan said. "Speak your piece."

Madison waited a few moments, and then arched his chest, flexing his muscles. He spread his feet, put his hands on his hips and began slowly. "My name is Bula Matadi... Bula Matadi... I am a breaker of stones. My African blood inspires me. Freedom is my birthright."

The three inquisitors stepped back. "I have a loaded pistol," Bascombe said.

"Ha!" Madison laughed, throwing his head back. "You will not shoot me. You would be denied your hanging spectacle."

"Trust me," Bascombe said, I will shoot." He pulled a dueling pistol from his waistband and pointed it at Madison's chest.

"Shoot if you are so inclined, but you could not harm me anymore than what you have already done."

"I never laid eyes on you before."

"For two hundred years you have enslaved my people. You will burn in hell for the misery you have brought upon the African. The Lord has promised it."

"And what would you heathens know of the Lord?" Bascombe asked.

"We also worship the God of Abraham."

"You are empty vessels, without souls.... that is why God made you slaves."

Madison stabbed Consul Bascombe with his eyes. "It is not His will that we should live under such oppression, but only the desires of the white man. Whose authority should we live by, you hypocrites? God's or man's?"

"You blaspheme! You won't get to a hanging."

Bascombe waved his pistol.

John Burnham palmed the muzzle toward the floor. "Give him his due."

Madison inhaled deeply. "Our mutiny only concerns you, Consul Bascombe, because you wish to curry favor with your own government. The truth is not a concern to you."

"How dare you speak for me!"

"We are only a cargo of flesh to you; slaves whom you refuse to set free as English law demands."

Burnham nodded his head, but Consul Bascombe cursed Madison again. "The law...? It does not apply to slaves, and you are only that... nothing more."

"Our time has come, there shall be many more uprisings."

"What do you mean; how would you know that?" Burnham asked.

"Fools! When word of our insurrection reaches the pens at Richmond, and then echoes across the Forks of the Road, and everywhere else that Africans are held in bondage, there will be a thousand such uprisings. Many will die, but we will be free!"

"That may be," Bascombe interrupted. "But you, Sir, will be dead... hanging from a cypress tree. By God's design you are a slave and you will die a slave."

Madison was undeterred. Inspired by the energy of his own oratory, he flailed his arms, like a pulpit preacher. He thought of Miss Agnes. He rememberd Shylock... "God made me a slave? No, it is the immoral force of the white man... overseers and their whips... that make us slaves."

Bascombe muttered, "As it should be."

Madison calmed. "Consul Bascombe, do you not

understand that Africans are human beings?" He held out his forearm. "See, if you pinch me, I also bleed."

"Purely a physical reaction."

"Beyond the physical... know ye that we have thoughts, feelings, passions and intelligence. Like the white man, our hearts also swell with love and can burn with hate. We ache with the sorrows... the misery you have brought upon us. Our souls boil for vengeance—"

"Revenge? You see, you speak of violence. You Negros must be shackled."

"It is true, Consul Bascombe.... Our passions are not so gentle... because you have made us this way. With your whips you scar our flesh and then wonder why we rebel. You forbid us to read and learn, and then you call us ignorant."

A small crowd of black men and women gathered near the door, listening to Madison's oratory. The women held hands and the men beamed at each other.

Bascombe spat on the floor. "You Negroes have no feelings except for violence."

"Considering the nature of our bondage, it should not surprise you that we are angry."

"Reason enough to keep you bound," Bascombe argued.

"It is natural... any enslaved man will seize liberty by force when the chance presents itself," Madison countered.

Robert Duncan's mouth was wide open. "Enough of this. Are you finished?"

"You may silence me, but you will hear from my people."

"I doubt that," Duncan said. "Your American masters seem to have a tight hold over all of you."

"That will change. When we struck out from the Creole, we rebelled for all slaves. Our fight is their fight. It is provoked by the conditions of our long enslavement... stirred by the removal of our children from their mothers; the separation of husbands from their wives, friends from friends. Hold this in your hearts: Slavery is against the laws of God. You will come to understand this as you look up at Heaven from the fires of hell!"

"Be that as it may, Mr. Washington," Bascombe said. "However, your fate is in my hands." He smiled and slapped the pistol against his palm.

"I do not worry about my fate, only that my children... that their children shall live in freedom."

"That might take a long time," John Burnham said. "How long are you prepared to wait?"

Madison raised himself to his full height. "A year... a hundred years.... Forever if necessary."

Madison was taken back to the hold. Burnham touched him on the shoulder as he passed through the admiring crowd.

Chapter Twenty-Seven

The Authorities Scheme

It became clear to the Americans that the British authorities in Nassau were not going to forward the former slaves to the United States. As events unfolded around them, Madison and his coconspirators remained in custody. They considered plans for escape should circumstances require it of them. They had not come this far to fail.

Consul Bascombe was frustrated at the attitude of the British authorities. He'd be held accountable by his superiors in Washington, he was sure. He consequently formulated a plan to bring an American warship to Nassau and take over the brig Creole. They would return her and the cargoes to American shores.

Captain Maximally Woodson was master of the American bark *Louisa*. She lay idle in the same harbor. He came aboard the Creole a few hours after she reached Nassau. Consul Bascombe invited him to come ashore and join him his office. There, he and several of his crew, along with the second mate and four men from the American Brig *Congress*, schemed with Bascombe to seize the Creole from the British officers. Captain Ingram and First Mate Gibson were present. Bascombe and Captain Woodson sat in large overstuffed chairs. "Can you regain control of this ship?" Bascombe asked.

Captain Woodson answered: "Without a doubt, Sir. The slaves will buckle quickly. We'll need firearms."

"Try not to spill any blood. These British—"

"There may be some disorder, but no killing."

"How will you accomplish this?"

"A simple show of force... with arms. After we seize her, we'll sail to Stirrup Key. An American warship is anchored there. The Marines will assist us."

Consul Bascombe asked Captain Ingram and Gibson for their views. Ingram, still convalescing from his wounds, approved of the plot. Gibson would become the captain of the Creole during Ingram's incapacitation.

"If you have these muskets... pistols and ammunition," Bascombe asked them, "are you certain your crews will assist us?"

Gibson and Ingram both assured Bascombe that their sailors were loyal and would fight to regain control of the Creole.

"We need to smuggle the arms on board, perhaps in luggage chests or something." Bascombe said. "You two will have to initiate the confrontation with the British military. I'd be dismissed if the Governor knew."

"And how do you suppose the British guard will react?" Captain Woodson wanted to know. "Should we fire upon them if they protest?"

"Good heavens, man." Bascombe retorted. "That might cause another war. You said that a display of arms would be sufficient."

"Where are these weapons?" Gibson asked.

Consul Bascombe counted out some cash and pushed it across his desk to Gibson. "There are arms shops in Freeport. Purchase them there."

Gibson and two of his sailors went into Freeport at Nassau. Unfamiliar with the streets, they inquired of several persons where arms were sold. At the first shop, the black owner rebuffed them. "Get out of my store, you evil slavers!" he demanded.

Gibson called at two more gun stores with similar results. At noon, he reported to Consul Bascombe. "We can't buy arms in Freeport."

"Why is that?" Bascombe asked.

"No one will sell us any weapons. When we walked in the streets, the locals cursed us and called us pirates and slavers. Even the children threw stones. We were damned lucky to get out of there."

"We'll find another way," Bascombe replied. We'll wait until after the military guard has been removed... see what happens."

On Friday morning, Police Magistrate Duncan entered Consul Bascombe's office. He informed him that the examination of witnesses was concluded. "A decision had been made by the Council. The passengers will be freed, but the nineteen accused murderers will be held for further examination."

"How can they conclude the investigation! Why, Captain Ingram has not given his testimony."

"We must conclude this Creole business."

"Why such haste?"

"There is much unrest in the city. Some sailors tried to buy weapons. Our citizens believe the slaves will be returned to their American owners by force. They won't have it."

"What can they do about it?"

"Citizens of both races are scheming to rescue the slaves and bring them to shore." Duncan said. He pointed out the window: "See that launch... the other small vessels near the Creole?"

"Yes.... What the hell are they doing?" Bascombe seethed.

"They are going to remove the slaves. You seem to be checkmated, Mr. Bascombe."

Bascombe, now furious, rushed off to inform the Governor General of the impending assault on the Creole.

A large crowd gathered on the shore. The people of Nassau were outraged that Africans were being held against their will. They saw it as a breach of the British law that guaranteed their own freedom. If these slaves were to be incarcerated at Nassau, or returned to the United States, then what did the future hold for their own liberties.

From the rail, the Creole crew watched the gathering crowd load into small boats. They collected clubs to defend themselves.

A dozen small boats, filled with angry men and women, made their way out to the Creole and surrounded it. Lieutenant Manson shouted: "Keep off or I will order my men to shoot." His guards stood ready at the rail, although he knew that he could not fire into the mob without justification.

Consul Bascombe asked to be taken to the Creole. With Robert Duncan, he raced down the pier and climbed the gangway. On board, he gathered the white Americans and briefed them. "Surely, the British authorities are provoking this mob. I believe they hired all these boats and people. They intend to free the slaves and murderers. You must stop it."

"Look, there's a Negro woman putting on her bonnet as if she's going somewhere," Duncan said. He pointed to several women stacking bags on the deck. "Look there, they're packing."

"We must find a way to stop them," Bascombe bellowed. "The British cannot free these slaves. There will be war!"

Alongside the Creole, the flotilla of angry men grew larger and louder. The man in the lead vessel shouted, "Get your business done; we are coming up to do ours."

Stevenson recognized him as the pilot who had steered the Creole to the dock. "We're waiting for Consul Bascombe, we'll be leaving then," he shouted over the rail.

The pilot yelled back, "Liar! Mr. Bascombe is aboard. You'd better take care of your valuables if you have any. No telling what our people might do when they come up."

"Damn," Merkle said. "As soon as the troopers are gone, they'll storm the ship."

The talk frightened the white passengers. One crewmember put on four pairs of pantaloons and another put on two suits as protection against being cut. They locked their trunks and put their money in their pockets. A stalemate ensued. Consul Bascombe returned to shore and hurried to the Governor's office, informing him of the irate crowd surrounding the Creole.

"I doubt that any of Her Majesty's subjects would act so improperly as to force their way aboard your ship," Sir Francis said. "They are law abiding citizens."

"They're an unruly mob," Bascombe argued.

Sir Francis replied: "You overstate the circumstances, Sir"

"I saw them with my own eyes."

"I assure you, Consul, that our citizens will not commit any violence."

"Sir, the officers and crew fear for their safety. Even the slaves are frightened."

"I remind you, Consul, those are passengers on that ship. Not slaves."

Bascombe grew angry. "I beg your pardon, Governor, but those Negroes are as much a part of the cargo as is the tobacco and cotton!"

"You try my patience, Consul. They are human beings, not cotton... not tobacco. Your ridiculous argument has no validity here. Now, I have issued certain directives. The Attorney General has been sent to the Creole with instructions to prevent any violence on the part of those surrounding the vessel. He will resolve that issue, as he is the chief law officer here."

"Thank you for that."

Sir Francis frowned, paused for a moment, and then continued. "Furthermore, Attorney General Andrews will escort the passengers from the Creole. They will be housed in local homes and churches while a disposition is made of their status. As you know, we are in somewhat vituperative communications with your government."

Consul Bascombe was stunned. "And the damned pirates... the murderers? Surely you will not release them into the population?"

"Andrews has been instructed to remove all of the passengers. The nineteen alleged mutineers will be held in administrative custody until we hear from England. Parliament is being made aware, and the affair is under discussion in Washington."

Bascombe departed. He did not want to arouse his host's ire any further, perhaps causing him to add to the guard. He went to the dock where he met Gibson and Captain Ingram. "Go on board the Creole immediately," Bascombe said. "You must protest every act of the Nassau Attorney General if he tries to deny you control of the slaves."

Gibson and Ingram immediately secured a small boat and headed toward the Creole. They were frightened by the mob and wondered if they would be allowed to pass. As they approached, the Attorney General shouted to the boats below to refrain from any acts of violence. "Let them aboard. When you see the passengers assembled on the quarter deck, come alongside and take them to shore."

The former slaves assembled on the deck and Attorney General Andrews addressed them. "Listen carefully. There are nineteen of you who have been identified as having been engaged in the murder of Mr. Howard and in an attempt to kill the captain and others. You individuals will be held in temporary detention while we communicate with our government as to whether a trial will take place here or elsewhere."

He further informed them that they would be provided counsel and they could review any documents in evidence against them. He then spoke to the other passengers.

"Friends, you have been detained aboard the brig Creole for the purpose of ascertaining the individuals concerned with mutiny and murder. They have been identified. The rest of you are at liberty to go ashore and do whatever you please."

No sounds of jubilation rose from the former slaves. They did not want to act in any way that might change the mind of the Attorney General. Freedom was just a few steps away.

Merkle approached Attorney General Andrews.

"Sir, might I mention to them that they are also free to return to the United States? Slaves are generally loyal to their owners."

"I doubt that, Mr. Merkle, but go ahead."

Merkle announced that anyone who wished to remain on board could do so. The former slaves looked at him in disbelief.

Attorney General Andrews left the ship in a small boat and pulled several yards away to watch and see if his instructions would be followed. He signaled to one of the officers on deck. The surrounding craft rushed in and bumped against the larger vessel. The passengers either climbed down ropes or jumped into the water and were pulled aboard the smaller craft. They were eager to get off the Creole and to enter freedom for the first time in their lives. Women and children were hurriedly escorted down the gangway. When everyone was ashore, on the dock, loud cheers went up from the crowd. The Attorney General went throughout the throng shaking hands with each person. He was told that five slaves had chosen to remain aboard.

"They refuse to accept their liberty," one of his officers told him.

"At what price... at what ungodly price," George Andrews remarked.

Gibson and the crew, intimidated by the Attorney General, made no protest as to the release of the slaves. "It's not worth it," Gibson said to Merkle and Stevenson. "It's out of our hands."

Consul Bascombe watched from the window of his office. He saw a large crowd of several thousand people gathering around the public buildings and government offices. Among them he saw the Creole slaves going into the office of the Inspector of Police, John Pinkston. Pinkston later told Bascombe that he had registered the names of the slaves and their occupations. "Your effort to return the slaves would have been in vain, Mr. Bascombe. Our people would never have permitted them to leave."

The following day, Gibson, Merkle, Stevenson, and Ingram met with Bascombe. Together they drafted a protest to the Governor General. Basically, they wrote that the "proceedings of Her Majesty's officers in liberating American slaves on British land was an illegal act and might have the probable consequences of war." Bascombe demanded that the nineteen prisoners be forwarded to the United States in the brig Creole. He envisioned American Marines landing and taking the slaves to New Orleans. Maybe they'd seize the entire island and he would become the Governor General.

Governor Cochoran sent back a rather curt reply, expressing his disappointment in the tone and content of Bascombe's letter. Sir Francis stated that the Consul's attitude was in direct contrast to what he had believed about Bascombe; that he was a sensible man and a seasoned diplomat. "Nonetheless," Sir Francis wrote: "Your request that the nineteen persons who have been implicated in the murder committed aboard the Creole, while at sea, should be delivered over to you for the purpose of trial in America is denied. I refer you to the document already furnished by my office that the parties in question shall be detained here until instructions are received from Her Majesty's government."

Consul Bascombe was crestfallen. He prepared testimony for his superiors in Washington.

Chapter Twenty-Eight

The Trial

Madison and the other eighteen identified mutineers were held in relatively unrestrained confinement. They were allowed the freedom of outdoor gardens and were not further interrogated. They, like their English hosts, awaited the decision of Her Majesty's government. Dr. Ruffin joked that he rather liked the term, Her Majesty. "I'd rather be under some woman, anytime."

Gibson, Merkle, Stevenson, and Captain Ingram likewise awaited instructions from America. On Monday, November 15, they received a dispatch from the owners of the Creole to set sail for New Orleans. They were to sell all unnecessary provisions to finance the trip and bring back as many slaves as they could. "By force of arms, if necessary," the letter read. Gibson tore it into shreds. "Prepare to sail very soon," he told the others. He did not mention the full contents of the note.

The next day Gibson tried to sell the ship's provisions of beef, pork, and navy bread. The collector of customs refused to grant him permission to land the goods unless he listed the Creole slaves as passengers, rather than slaves, on the ship's manifests. "And bring their baggage to shore as quickly as possible," the customs agent said.

"I will not," Gibson answered.

"So, you refuse? Then you may not land your stocks, Mr. Gibson."

Consul Bascombe, back in his office, was informed that another ship, the *Francis Cochoran*, would sail to Jamaica within a few days with certain "emigrants."

The Creole cleared Nassau, bound for New Orleans, on Thursday, November 18, 1841, as Bascombe watched from the shore. Only the five returning slaves and crew were aboard. Immediately thereafter, the *Francis Cochoran* glided out of the same harbor, bound for Jamaica, with more than fifty, free blacks from the Creole. They would spend the reminder of their lives in Jamaica and among other islands of the Caribbean. Some of them prospered, others did not. Regardless of the futures they established for themselves and the places they opted to live, this is certain: they breathed free air and labored at tasks that they chose to perform. They never felt a whip again.

In New Orleans, the news made headlines in every newspaper and bulletin. Southerners were outraged that the slaves had been freed. The *Courrier da la Louisiana* printed an editorial stating, "...that insolent and intolerable meddler, John Bull, must be held responsible. And should he persist in his outrageous course, there can be no other alternative left, but for the American Eagle to make such a noise about his ears, as will awaken him from his fancied security..."

Madison and his friends were unaware that they had brought England and America to a fever pitch of scathing accusations, bordering on declarations of war. They idled away their time, planning their futures and acclimating themselves to the Bahamas.

Several days after news accounts of the mutiny and British refusal to surrender the slaves swept across America, President John Tyler rebuked England in the national newspapers. He wrote: "Our position is that illegal force and murdering violence can give no jurisdiction to England over property or persons belonging to the United States; that the Creole, under the circumstances, was as much within the jurisdiction of the United States as if it were in our own waters. Neither the slaves on board nor the murderers were amenable to British laws or British seizure; when, therefore, the officers at Nassau entered this vessel, and took from thence the mutineers and murderers. They committed as gross an outrage on the sovereignty of the United States as if they had sent an expedition to the shores of Virginia, and taken them from a jail in Norfolk. The whole question is one of mere power; and the nation that cannot enforce its own rights, it may be assured, will never have them respected by other nations."

An impressive adobe building, built for traveling merchants and sailors served as a prison for Madison and the other accused murderers. It was formerly an inn, with plenty of rooms, toilet facilities, and a large kitchen. Within, the atmosphere among the mutineers was congenial and relaxed. Milinda and Isaac visited Madison every afternoon and evening. She and Isaac were guests of a family who had themselves escaped slavery a few years before. "I'm working around the house and in the garden," she told Madison. "Someday we'll have a place just like it. I wish the Queen would answer... I need you."

Madison wanted to hold her close and would have done so, except for the attention little Isaac demanded.

He carried the tot on his shoulders, parading him around the large community room, showing him off to all his friends. Many remarked that he was a handsome child and "very special."

"You sure is getting' big... and smart like your daddy," Elijah Morris said.

Other women and men from the Creole, now living as free people, brought food, fruit and necessities to the prisoners. Occasionally, a spontaneous prayer meeting developed and Madison preached on the value of the human soul and man's inherent dignity. Someone remarked that Madison had missed his calling.

"You will be a fine preacher when you are free, Madison," Martha Thompson remarked. "We'll all come to your church... might even drop a shilling or two on the plate." Martha was one of the Creole slaves who had not resettled on another island. She claimed to like Nassau, and was planning to become a British citizen.

The weeks became months and gradually the former slaves of the Creole assimilated into Nassau society. They become thriving and content, except for the nagging fear that Madison and the other prisoners might somehow suffer for having led them to freedom. In some houses, plans were developing for freeing the nineteen if the British courts decided to punish them.

Milinda led the cause: "We made it to freedom before, and we can do it again. Madison will be free or I'll take my place on the gallows beside him."

Madison hardly noticed the winter of 1841. He recalled the cold Canadian winds and the Bahamian climate pleased him more. It was an unusually cool evening in February 1842, when Attorney General George Andrews called upon the lodge where Madison and his cohorts were sheltered. He declined to sit, and asked if all nineteen mutineers were present. They gathered around him, some sitting on the floor, others finding benches or chairs.

The Attorney General paused, and then cleared his throat: "Gentlemen, It is no secret that I sympathize with your predicament. If I could set you all free, believe me, I would do so. But—"

"Ah, here it comes," Elijah Morris interrupted. What did the Queen say, she gonna' boil us in oil?"

"You are remarkably perceptive, Mr. Morris. There is grim news from England, but not from the Queen. She has yet to speak on the matter."

"Grim news?" Madison asked.

Attorney General Andrews drew a breath. "There are issues of which you are unaware. Your case is now an international dispute. Certain treaties... boundaries... are being threatened because of it. A number of English diplomats would rather appease the Americans."

"What does this mean to us," Madison asked.

"Have you heard of our Prime Minister, Lord Melbourne?"

"Can't say that I have," Dr. Ruffin chimed in.

"He's under tremendous pressure to resolve the situation. He's a bit of a spineless chap; not much stomach for argument. As a gesture to the Americans, he has ordered that you stand trial for murder. The briefs are being prepared now."

"I knew we'd all hang," Ben Johnson said. "Who would defend us?"

Attorney General Anderson replied: "It would please me to serve as your counsel, Gentlemen. I have the court's permission. The trial will take place in a few weeks. We have much to discuss before then."

"What is there to talk about," Madison said. "Bascombe and Duncan have already condemned us. How would you defend us?"

"I will try. I continue to believe that our young queen will speak on the matter. Unfortunately, she has been under the influence of Lord Melbourne. She married recently and they say she's beginning to show a spark of independence."

"So, the Prime Minister been in bed with the Queen?" Dr. Ruffin said. "He ordered the trial? And you think she gonna' cut us loose?"

"I will do my best to represent you. Now give me the true specifics of the mutiny, all of it."

Attorney General Andrews took a seat at the table. He opened a leather binder and prepared to write. By midnight, he had all of the facts regarding the Creole rebellion. He snapped his binder closed. "I will see you in court, Gentlemen."

Twenty-nine year old George C. Andrews was a Scot, born in Edinburgh, and educated in private schools, a benefit of his family's wealth. George was a homely child, having survived an early bout of chicken pox, which left his face slightly scared and pock marked. He avoided contact with his youthful peers and spent most of his time reading scholarly works. At sixteen, he was awarded a scholarship to the Edinburgh School of Law, graduating with honors and immediately entering the British Foreign Service. He excelled at looking after the Empire's interests at postings in India and Australia, serving as an auditor of finances and later a prosecutor. In July 1840, he was offered the Attorney General's chair in Nassau, an opportunity that he gladly seized. Nassau was known to be peaceful; its citizens loyal to the crown, and the climate would suit him.

He had been the Attorney General for little more than a year when he met Madison Washington.

Lord George Abernathy, a senior magistrate of the Admiralty, was dispatched from England to hear the case of the Creole Mutineers. Three weeks at sea made the white-haired, stoop-shouldered judge angry at the whole affair. Chilled to the bone from the late winter passage, he preferred to be back in England, sitting by his fireplace. He had little sympathy for the Negro race and the liberal social movements sweeping across Great Britain at the time. "Brief me, set a quick trial date, and let's dispose of this mess," he told John Boyle, a young Nassau prosecutor assigned to the case. "I intend to be back in England before the end of the month."

Attorney General Andrews visited Madison and the accused mutineers several more times during the days before the trial. "Lord Abernathy is impatient," he told the group. He seems to have already decided your fate. Carpenters are building gallows as we speak."

At five o'clock in the morning on March 15, Lieutenant Manson, along with six armed guards, escorted Madison and the prisoners through the darkened streets of Freeport. Milinda and a few other women walked beside them, but no physical contact was allowed. Lieutenant Manson enforced absolute silence: "Lest the citizens be awakened and cause a ruckus."

They arrived at the small courthouse before daylight and were ushered into pews. Consul Bascombe, John Burnham, and Robert Duncan arrived shortly thereafter. Only Burnham looked at the accused and nodded. Defense Counsel Andrews arrived and quietly took a seat at the defense's table. He looked at Madison briefly, and then turned to his notes.

Several clerks and assistants arrived at the courtroom just as daylight beamed through the arched, stained glass windows. They placed legal briefs on desks and otherwise prepared for trial. At precisely eight o'clock, Lord Abernathy and two additional black-robed judges entered from a rear doorway and took their seats on the bench. Lord Abernathy adjusted his white powdered wig and cleared his throat. He uttered a quick prayer asking for wisdom, and then made a short reference to the queen. Finally, he addressed the court.

"Please be seated, Gentleman. You know precisely why we are assembled here. In the event there is someone amongst you that does not, I'll explain. As senior judge for Her Majesty's Admiralty Court, I am authorized to conduct this trial and take whatever action I deem appropriate. There will be no jury. The accused persons will stand. Clerk, read the charges."

The court clerk strode to the podium and faced the nineteen prisoners. They stood erect, not bowing or otherwise showing emotion. He read: "The following named individuals are accused of the premeditated murder of one Mr. John R. Howard aboard the American Brig Creole, while at sea, on the night of November seven, in the year of Our Lord, one-thousand, eight-hundred and forty one, by thrusting a knife into the bosom of the aforementioned Mr. Howard, thereby causing his death." He read the names of Madison Washington and all accused, and then concluded by asking: "How say ye? Guilty or not guilty."

George Andrews stood beside the prisoners. "Not guilty, your Lordship."

"Be seated, Andrews. Now, Mr. Boyle, present the Crown's case," Lord Abernathy commanded.

John Boyle faced the accused and then turned

toward the three judges. "If it might please the court, after an exhaustive examination of witnesses aboard the Brig Creole at the time of the mutiny, it has been established that all of the accused had a hand in the killing of Mr. Howard, as either the actual killer, or as an accessory to the slaying. I will prove that to the satisfaction of all."

"Proceed," Lord Abernathy said.

"I call to the witness stand, Lieutenant Manson of Her Majesty's Royal Light Guard Brigade."

Lieutenant Manson, dressed in a formal red and black uniform, strode quickly to the witness stand. He held his saber at his side and stood at attention. "Present, Sir!"

"Please be at ease, Lieutenant Manson. I won't keep you long," Prosecutor Boyle said. "Lieutenant, did you participate in the investigation of the murder of Mr. Howard? Did you conduct interviews?"

"Yes, Sir. I interviewed not only the accused, but every passenger aboard the Creole."

"And your findings?"

Lieutenant Manson pointed at the accused. "Each of the prisoners seated there admitted to thrusting the knife into Mr. Howard."

"Would you therefore conclude that at least one, if not several of them had a hand in the slaying?"

"Indeed I would."

"Thank you. I am finished with this witness, Your Lordship."

Lord Abernathy did not look up. "You may examine the witness, Mr. Andrews."

George Andrews rose slowly. He removed his long coat, folded it and placed it over his chair. He walked back and forth in front of Lieutenant Manson several times, staring at the floor and snapping his suspenders from time to time. A hint of gray reflected off his hair and to those who knew him, he appeared much older than his twenty-nine years.

"Lieutenant Manson, through your interviews, were you able to ascertain who the actual killer or killers were?"

"Not exactly, but I believe that amongst them is the killer."

"Your opinion is not called for, Lieutenant, but I'll disregard that." George Andrews waved his hand, paced a few more steps and addressed his witness again. "Tell me, Lieutenant, what police training have you had, if any, regarding the conduct of criminal investigations?"

Lieutenant Manson's faced flushed. "Any officer of Her Majesty's guards may conduct an investigation. It is necessary to good order."

"By 'good order', you mean inquiries about barracks thefts, disobedience, such things as that?"

"Yes, Sir."

"Have you ever conducted a murder investigation... before the Creole affair?"

"No, Sir."

"I ask you again, Lieutenant Manson, what police training have you had, what academies?"

Lieutenant Manson exploded. "You question my professionalism, Sir. I am well trained—"

"Please name the school. Again, what police academies or schools prepared you for this investigation?"

"None, Sir!"

"You may step down."

Lord Abernathy scowled at George Andrews. "Mr. Boyle, call your next witness."

The prosecutor called for Robert Duncan. He

took his post at the witness podium and looked at the growing audience of black faces. Inwardly, he considered the possibility of violence. "Robert Duncan is present, Sir."

"Mr. Duncan, I understand that you are the Police Magistrate for Nassau. Is that correct?"

"Yes."

"How long have you held this post?"

"Five years, approximately. And, I studied at the Royal Police Academy in London, I am well—"

"Spare us, Mr. Duncan." I am familiar with your background. Did you conduct an investigation aboard the Creole?"

"Yes, I did. An exhaustive inquiry, I might add."

"Your findings?"

"Of all who confessed, I managed to boil it all down to one man."

"And that man is?"

"Madison Washington, the ring leader." Duncan shot an accusing finger at Madison. "He calls himself by some African name, 'Bula Matadi' I believe he said."

"And you believe that he alone committed the act of murderer."

"Yes!"

"Why is that? What evidence do you offer to support such a claim?"

"He was certainly the most persuasive of all the witnesses... quite eloquent I must say. The others spoke gibberish."

"Your witness, Mr. Andrews."

George Andrews looked quizzically at Robert Duncan. "Oh, so he described the killing, the location on deck? Did he explain how he came by the knife, at what angle he thrust it into Mr. Howard?"

"Not exactly. It wouldn't matter, the body was thrown overboard."

"Mr. Duncan, surely in your vast experience, you learned that there are minute details to any crime that only the perpetrator would know. What details did Mr. Washington provide? Tell us."

"He said, "I thrust the knife into Mr. Howard." That was good enough for me.'"

"But he gave no details?"

"No."

"I ask you, did anyone else confess to the crime?"

Magistrate Duncan was hesitant to answer immediately."Mr. Duncan, I insist that you answer the question. Did any one of the accused, or anyone at all aboard that ship, also confess to the killing?"

Duncan reply was almost inaudible. "Yes, Sir.

"Who was it then... who confessed? Please tell the court."

"The fellow they call Elijah, and then there was that slave, Dr. Ruffin."

Defense Counsel Andrews frowned at the remark. He raised his voice, almost shouting. "Is it not true, Mr. Duncan, that every mutineer... and every former slave aboard the Creole confessed to the killing?"

Duncan let out a sigh. "Indeed, it is true, Sir. But I—

"You are dismissed, Mr. Duncan."

Prosecutor Boyle rushed forward to protest, but Magistrate Duncan was already leaving the witness stand and George Andrews was seated.

Boyle called John Burnham to the stand. "What is your position in the colony, Sir?"

"I am the Justice of The Peace."

"You also took part in the investigation. What were your conclusions?"

"I drew no conclusions. I also have investigative training and this one leaves us without much fact. We do not have the weapon, we have no body for examination or comparisons—"

Robert Duncan's answer alarmed the prosecutor. He silently wished that he had previously interviewed Mr. Duncan at greater length. He had no choice but to continue:"Did you hear anyone else confess to the slaying?"

"Oh, yes... several... this fellow, Ben Johnson and the others Duncan mentioned. They all admitted to the crime."

Prosecutor Boyle wiped his brow. "Are you saying that you cannot even offer an assumption...?"

"Yes, I am as perplexed now as I was during the interrogations. I cannot say with any certainty as to who, specifically, killed Mr. Howard."

"No idea at all? Why is that?" The prosecutor thundered.

"Lack of evidence, Sir."

John Boyle stopped abruptly. "I am finished with this witness."

Lord Abernathy looked quizzically at the prosecutor and shook his head. "Mr. Andrews..."

"I decline to interview Mr. Burnham, thank you," George Andrews said.

Lord Abernathy spoke impatiently. "Mr. Boyle, have you any other evidence to present to this court?"

"There is also the written testimony of one Mr. Joseph Ligonier, but he has sailed for America," Boyle replied.

"Let us see what he had to say," Lord Abernathy said. Prosecutor Boyle handed him Ligonier's statement. He read it briefly and then handed it to the judge on his right. "It looks conclusive to me."

Lord Abernathy addressed both the defense and prosecution counsels. Do either of you have anything else to say before we deliberate the matter?"

"Nothing, Your Lordship," Boyle said. "I rest my case."

George Andrews rose again. "If it pleases the court. I ask your indulgence for a moment. I submit that no evidence has been presented here that would definitively identify any one murderer. I ask that you dismiss this case."

"On what grounds?" Lord Abernathy seethed. We have plenty of testimony..."

"This testimony is nothing but hearsay, conjecture and outright lies. No reliable evidence of who killed Mr. Howard has been presented."

Judge Abernathy fumed. "He was killed during the uprising.... One of them damn sure did it! Their statements show that clearly."

George Andrews digested Judge Abernathy's veiled threat to punish them all, thereby including the actual murderer. "Is it not better to free one guilty man, lest other innocents suffer? Is that not English law?" George Andrews roared.

"Well spoken, Mr. Andrews," Lord Abernathy replied. "But I have all the facts I need. We'll retire to chambers and render our findings later in the day. This court is in recess." He stood, banged his gavel several times, collected some papers and entered an anteroom along with the other judges. They sat in comfortable over-stuffed chairs and drank refreshments.

Charles Frazier, the youngest judge, removed his wig and opened the collar of his robes. "Andrews made a good point. I don't see how we can decide anything with such flimsy evidence."

"I agree," Phillip Boykin, the other judge said. "We can't hang or imprison anyone on this testimony. It's all tittle-tattle... unsubstantiated... conspiratorial admissions of guilt. They all confess to murder to protect the guilty one."

Lord Abernathy took his time. He sipped on his drink, and then set it on a table. "Gentlemen, there are certain facts of which you are unaware: the first of them being that I did not cross the icy North Atlantic to bring home a dismissal. I have instructions from the Prime Minister."

"The PM does not dictate the decisions of the courts," Judge Boykin said. "That would profane—"

Lord Abernathy stood up. "Have either of you heard of the Ashburton-Webster treaty?"

"Yes, I believe those negotiations are under way in Washington," Judge Boykin replied. "Lord Ashburton is discussing America's territorial claims to Maine. Seems they'll have all of Canada before long."

"Correct," Lord Abernathy said. "After a long running dispute over our boundaries, an agreement between Lord Ashburton and Secretary of State Daniel Webster has been reached. It awaits Senate ratification. Therein lies the problem."

"What problem?" Charles Frazier asked.

"The Creole affair, it threatens to shatter this delicate agreement. The American slave owners dominate their congress. They demand retribution. They're threatening to tar and feather Lord Ashburton and send him home."

"Gracious," Judge Boykin remarked.

"I have my instructions from the Prime Minister. We will hang several of the mutineers; imprison the rest for a time. England will pay compensation for each slave lost. That should satisfy the Americans."

"I refuse to be a part of this horrid sham," Charles Frazier said. "I can't believe it."

Lord Abernathy took another sip of his drink. He stared at Frazier and then Boykin. "You'll go along with it or you will both spend the rest of your careers shuffling papers in the cold cellars of parliament. I have the authority, you know."

A gloomy silence filled the room. No one spoke for several moments. Finally, Charles Frazier stood and buttoned his robes. "Let's bring the guilty parties in."

Chapter Twenty-Nine

Judgment Day

In London, twenty-two year old Queen Victoria summoned Prime Minister Lord Melbourne to her offices. Her new husband, German Prince Albert of Saxe-Coburg-Gotha was present when the Prime Minister entered. Lord Melbourne bowed, and then kissed her extended hand. "It is so good to see you again, Your Majesty. It has been too long—"

"It most certainly has," the young queen replied. "I've missed your counsel. ...so good of you to come."

Prince Albert joined the Queen at her side. "Welcome, Lord Melbourne, please take a seat. Victoria and I have been discussing matters from abroad. You know I've just returned from America."

"Ah, well... since the wedding, you've both been so pre—"

"Preoccupied with each other?" Queen Victoria laughed. She sat on a large embroider settee and motioned Prince Albert to sit beside her. "I'll speak directly to the issue. What do you know of these former slaves now residing in Nassau? Albert tells me that there is much discussion about the affair in America. Has it actually disrupted Lord Ashburton's purposes there?"

"Precisely, Your Majesty. Ashburton could well loose our northern boundaries to the colony."

German Prince Albert bolted upright. "Ach! die Kolonie? You do not accepted their independence?"

"It's an old viewpoint... just a slip of the tongue, I assure you, Sir. But in the matter of the Creole and the slaves, I've issued instructions to our senior magistrate."

"And who might that be?" Queen Victoria asked.

"Lord Abernathy. He's in Nassau at this very moment conducting an inquiry. I believe we'll have the matter resolved to everyone's satisfaction in a matter of days."

"What, specifically, were your instructions to the Lord? I have some concerns..."

Prince Albert dismissed a servant and closed the door. "Wir müssen sprechen.... We must talk."

An hour passed before Queen Victoria bid farewell to Lord Melbourne. She handed him an envelope at the door. "Do make haste, Lord."

Lord Melbourne joined his secretary in a waiting carriage. "Take me to the Admiralty, immediately!"

"What is it, Lord Melbourne? You look ashen," his secretary observed.

"That damn German prince. Up her skirts all the time. He's got her hoodwinked. Oh, never mind! Locate our fastest ship and order the captain ready to sail."

In Nassau, the Creole murder trial reconvened at mid-afternoon. Spectators packed the courthouse, Milinda, Isaac, and Martha Thompson among them. Madison led the accused to their seats, stirring the air as he passed Milinda. She felt his heat, his presence, and clutched little Isaac to her bosom. "Pray hard for daddy," she whispered.

A stifling heat greeted the three judges as they emerged from behind closed doors. After some formalities, Lord Abernathy wiped his brow and ordered the accused to stand.

"We have concluded our deliberations... made a decision." He read from a sheaf of papers. "Mr. Washington, Mr. Morris, all of you... This court has weighed the facts of your case quite carefully. It is our opinion that the murder of Mr. Howard was committed by at least four of you. However, your attempt to shield the truth by each of you confessing to the murder has not blinded us. It is our believe that you, Mr. Madison Washington, ordered the slaying of Mr. Howard, or perhaps struck the fatal blow yourself. We also believe that Mr. Ruffin, Mr. Johnson, and Mr. Morris had a personal hand in it. You other mutineers are certainly accessories, as you tried to conceal evidence and confuse the court. You did not succeed." Lord Abernathy laid his notes on the desk.

George Andrews rose abruptly. "Lord Abernathy, I strongly protest your findings. No evidence has been presented here—"

"Sit down, Mr. Andrews. You had your chance. It is the decision of this court that Mr. Washington, Mr. Ruffin, Mr. Morris, and Mr. Johnson, shall all hang by the neck until dead. And you, Mr. Washington, or whatever you call yourself, will be the first to go. The execution date shall be set at a later hearing. The remainder of you will be imprisoned for a lengthy period of time. Twenty Five years at hard labor should serve to make you think more seriously about what you have done. This court is adjourned."

The judges hastily left the courtroom. Madison

and the others were escorted back to their lodgings and placed under heavy guard.

It was mid-April when Madison and his co-conspirators were awakened by an officer of the courts. "Gentlemen," he said. "Make yourselves presentable. You will appear before the Admiralty Court at nine o'clock."

Madison polled his friends: "Judgment day has arrived. Is anyone afraid?"

"Hell no," Ben Johnson said. "I'm a comin' to believe in that Jesus of yours."

"Just glad to be getting it over with... been too long," Dr. Ruffin said. A murmur of agreement rose from the incarcerated men. None of them voiced any fear, eager as they were to put an end to their long ordeal.

At 8:30 a.m., a half-dozen police guards arrived to escort the prisoners to the court chambers. The walk of about a half-mile was lined with several thousand inhabitants of the island and foreigners from many ports. American newspaper reporters from New Orleans, New York, and as far away as San Francisco watched from the sidelines. Politicians and bureaucrats from Washington and other major capitals of the world were present. They were anxious to witness the British government's response to American demands.

"I trust we'll have an early hanging," An observer said. It is so uncomfortably hot in the afternoons."

"I was hoping for at least one execution," a reporter from Jackson, Mississippi, replied. "Several hangings will be all the more satisfying to report."

The parade of prisoners took on a gala characteristic. Women and children cheered the mutineers as they marched along. Garlands of flowers were thrown at their feet and shouts of, "freedom... free our brothers," echoed from the crowds. Someone started playing a trumpet and soon a drum joined in. Eventually, a band of sorts led the entourage.

Madison walked hand in hand with Milinda, both of them proudly leading the procession. He carried Isaac on his shoulders and they waved to the adulating crowds as they passed.

"You're a hero to them, Madison," Milinda said. "I'm sure glad I snatched you back in that cornfield."

Madison squeezed her hand. "If I am to die... promise that you will have no others—"

"I will have no others because you won't be dead, my love. If they hang you, they must hang me. This whole colony will rise up in revolt. And the good Queen... she don't want that."

At precisely nine o'clock, the nineteen defendants filed into the courthouse. After courtesies to Charles Frazier, now the presiding judge, the audience fell silent. The clamor of shouting islanders blared though the walls and windows: "Free Bula Matadi, let him go, free our brothers, stop this show!" they chanted.

"Let's get this over with," Judge Frazier said. He handed a sheaf of papers to prosecutor Boyle who nervously fumbled the sheets, finally selecting one to read.

"By order of the Admiralty Court: It is the decision of this court that Mr. Madison Washington receive the sentence of death by hanging for the murder of Mr. John Howard. He is to be executed on this day, April 16, 1842, immediately following these proceedings. And then Mr. Ruffin, Mr. Johnson, and Mr. Morris will each hang on succeeding days, in that order, between sunrise and noon. The remaining prisoners will be escorted henceforth to the Royal Nassau prison, where they will be incarcerated for a period of no less than twenty-five years, no more than forty. God save the Queen!"

The courtroom exploded with vile curses for the British government. The spectators promised civil disobedience, riots, and rebellion. Milinda held Isaac close and tears streamed down her cheeks. Judge Frazier ordered the bailiffs to clear the courthouse. Outside, Lieutenant Manson and his guards established order. An eerie quiet descended over the crowd. The gallows loomed before them and the hangman prepared his noose.

Madison shuffled forward of the crowd and was unshackled. He immediately lunged toward Milinda and Isaac, embracing them mightily. "Cry not for me, my love. My destiny is fulfilled. I will see you at the foot of God's throne." He pushed her away and allowed two guards to escort him to the steps of the gallows. He quickly made his way onto the platform.

"Do you wish to be blindfolded," the hooded executioner asked.

"No, I wish to see the gates of Heaven open as my Lord receives me."

Madison turned toward the crowd, hoping to see and acknowledge Milinda and Isaac one last time. He scanned the assemblage, found her and Isaac, and mouthed, "I love you."

The executioner slipped the heavy hemp noose around Madison's neck and adjusted it. He then placed both his hands on Madison's shoulders and shook him gently, with a hint of affection. "You won't twist long, Mate. With your bulk, your neck will snap right quick. ...a minute, maybe two."

Madison, no longer wishing to burden Milinda, shifted his gaze upon the harbor. An unusual sight caught his attention. A large sailing vessel had recently moored at the docks. During the night, Madison thought. He could read her large colorful lettering. She was the *Britannia*. Powered by steam and sail, she was the fastest vessel on the seas. Sailors lowered the gangway and a tall man raced to the dock, mounted a waiting horse and galloped toward the center of town. Madison lost sight of him as he disappeared behind the buildings.

"Do you have any final words, Mr. Washington?" the hangman asked.

"I will mention you to Jesus."

The hangman ushered Madison over the trap-door and he felt it flex under his weight. He waited for its release; a moment that would liberate him from all his sorrows and send him into the arms of his God. He looked toward the sky, thinking little about the next few seconds. He was already in harmony with the afterworld.

Suddenly, a commotion broke out in the crowd, low at first, and then louder. The horseman galloped into their midst, drew up, and jumped from the steed. "Stop, stop this execution," he shouted. I have word from Her Majesty. Take me to the chief magistrate, immediately!"

A few brief comments passed between the messanger and Judge Frazier. He signaled the executioner to remove the rope from Madison's neck. "Bring the prisoner into the courtroom."

Madison descended the several steps and strode independently to the courtroom door. Like ants drawn to honey, the crowd followed him.

Judge Frazier demanded order. "What information do you have for this court, Sir? You say the Queen has sent a dispatch. What does it say?"

The rider reached into his satchel and produced

an engraved envelope with the royal seal embedded in wax. "I do not know what it says, it is sealed. My instructions were to halt any proceedings and to deliver the post to you. I do so now."

Judge Frazier opened the envelope and read the contents carefully. A faint smile creased his lips as he addressed George Andrews and handed him the letter. "Read it, and then explain it to the accused."

George Andrews perused the letter while Milinda and the onlookers collectively held their breaths. Andrews allowed the letter to drop to his side. "Please stand Mr. Washington, as the primary representative of the accused persons." Andrews cleared his throat, looked intently at Madison. He brought the letter before his eyes and said: "These are the principal points of interest by Her Majesty in your case of mutiny and murder. If you do not understand anything, please feel free to interrupt."

Andrews' hand shook, holding the message before him. His voice quivered slightly. He cleared his throat again and began: "Her Majesty's message reads: First: These persons held in bondage as slaves, had a natural and inalienable right to regain their freedom in the manner they did."

Again, unbridled pandemonium ensued in the crowded courtroom. Judge Frazier demanded order and rapped his gavel repeatedly.. Milinda, forced to sit in the rear, squeezed Martha Thompson's hand.

The Attorney General continued. "Second: British courts have no jurisdiction of the offenses, namely, 'mutiny and murder', when committed by aliens on board a vessel belonging to a foreign government."

Someone near the rear door raced out to inform the milling crowds and perhaps quell their aggitation..

The commotion caused Andrews to pause. "I'll continue Bailiff, if you can keep order in this court." He drew a breath and spoke directly to Madison.

"Third: This particular alleged crime of piracy and murder is viewed as follows: The only testimony which went to prove the charge of piracy was contained in the deposition of one Joseph Ligonier, and in regard to this man, it appeared that he was one of the persons who was most untrustworthy in his description of events in that he accused each of the principal mutineers, individually, without evidence or facts, totally contradicting the depositions given by the passengers of the vessel, who were not under suspicion, and thus, they were not predisposed to give false testimony. Therefore, his statement is without merit and is neither considered nor believed.

"Fourth: In the course of the investigation, it occurred that no less than ninety-seven passengers aboard the Creole confessed to the crime of murder and leading an insurrection; one of them a child as young as nine years of age; another a female of thirteen. It is therefore concluded that the entire investigation is pure poppycock, without substance and credibility—"

A cry went up from the audience, silencing the Attorney General until order was restored. Everyone stood, too energized to remain seated. Andrews stopped reading and then summarized. "After this declaration from the Queen, it is perhaps needless to add that the order to execute you and imprison your associates is null and void. You are exonerated of all alleged crimes by proclamation of Her Majesty, Queen Victoria. You are free to go and enjoy the blessings of liberty. Long live the Queen!"

Jubilation surged through the courtroom and outside. Madison shook the hand of George Andrews, and then hugged him. Judge Frazier smiled as he casually rapped his gavel for order.

With calm restored, Consul Bascombe rose and stated that he hoped that his part in the affair would not meet with censure. "I was only doing my duty," he said. Upon returning to his office he was handed a dispatch from Washington, recalling him and sending a replacement envoy. "Damn Negroes," he cursed. "They've ruined me"

Milinda did not wait until the courtroom settled down, She pushed forward, threw her arms around Madison and cried, "Oh, Madison, Madison… you are free… we are all free. Rebecca, God bless her, is redeemed, her prophecy fulfilled."

Madison smiled. "Yes, bless Rebecca and bless the good queen. ...and bless little Gopher."

"Who?"

"I'll tell you all about him someday. He was an angel sent from God." He gathered Milinda with one arm, Isaac with the other and kissed them both. Together they walked out the door into the embrace of the jubilant islanders and into a life of unending freedom.

EPILOGUE

Madison and Milinda remained in Nassau for several years as did many of the other former Creole slaves. Eventually they departed for other islands under the protection of the British crown. A few sailed to Liberia. Nassau records revealed that several families returned to Africa. Madison, Milinda, Isaac and their other children moved to St. Thomas in 1860. He earned his living as a dry goods merchant. He and Milinda had many more offspring. As the children grew older and found their own way in life, Madison felt a longing for his country of birth. His childhood memories of Rebecca, Charles and Ruth King, the sweet smelling earth of Mississippi and Louisiana, beckoned him home.

In 1869, Madison and Milinda and six of their children made their way to the United States, settling in Louisiana, near Bluff Creek, not too far from Clinton. Madison became a full time minister, a profession that suited him. He founded a Baptist church near Bluff Creek, where worshipers practice their faith today. In 1911, at the age of ninety-two, he died peacefully in his sleep.

After struggling out of bed that day, he visited the bathroom and read the local news. He inched his way into the living room and told his youngest great granddaughter that he had, "had enough." He was going to take a nap. He retired with a picture of Milinda in his right hand and a bible across his chest and he willed his life away. The coroner's investigation revealed that he had died of natural causes and he did not suffer. His living descendants numbered in the hundreds and his funeral was attended by a multitude of mourners. Some say they saw his soul going to Heaven as they laid him in the ground next to his mother, near Natchez, Mississippi.

Elisah Morris started an export company and shipped bananas to the people of the United States. He died of the flu in 1871. He fathered twenty-six children.

Ben Johnson hanged for the murder of a saloon keeper, only a few years after gaining his freedom.

Dr. Ruffin disappeared. Some say he fought in the Civil War.

John Armstead burned to death in his offices at the Forks of the Road. He had fallen asleep with a lighted cigar in his hand. Several dozen Negro slaves stood and watched the fire; some even fanning the flames. He left no heirs and his slaving business came to an abrupt halt. Union forces occupied his land in 1865 and turned it into a peanut farm.

Consul Bascombe suffered career losses in government service and at the polls when he ran for election in his home state of South Carolina. He took up the profession of a brick mason and eventually became a foreman. He died in a freak accident when a Negro laborer dropped a hopper full of bricks on his head from atop a scaffold.

In 1842, Thomas McCargo of Richmond, Virginia, experienced financial difficulty resulting from the loss of the Creole slaves. Authorities seized his entire estate. During the Civil War, Union Forces destroyed the McCargo plantation. Thomas McCargo and his son Theophilus, fled to New Orleans where they labored as woodcutters and mule drivers for several years. Thomas died with a chicken bone stuck in his throat. Theophilus was later arrested on a charge of pedophilia. He spent the few remaining years of his life in Angola prison, not far from Woodville, Mississippi.

In 1975, a committee of slave descendants from

Natchez placed a small cement marker at the spot where the roads forked. That is all that exists of it today.

The others involved in the life of Madison Washington and the Creole affair moved on to distant lands and other occupations. Their personal histories are lost to the passage of time. Their names, taken from the ship's manifest, follow. Please remember them well.

The Creole Slave Manifest

November 7, 1841

Caroline Andrews, Female, age 16

Andrew Bankhead, Male, age 25

Lucy Belam (or Beldon), Female, age 24

Adelaide Bell, Female, age 18

Hester Bell, Female, age 25

Lewis Bernard, Male, age 19

Horace Beverly, Male, age 19 *

A. Bird, Male, age 35

Ben Blair, Male, age 15

Mary Ann Boam, Female, age 17

George Brett, Male, age 19

Harry Brown, Male, age 21 *

Nelly Brown, Female, age 18

James Bruce, Male, age 18

William Bryant, Male, age 23

George Burton (or Burden), Male, age 19*

Benjamin Butler, Male, age 16

Richmond Butler, Male, age 23 *

Adam Carney, Male, age 23

C. Carter, Male, age 16

Lewis Carter, Male, age 18

Lucy Carter, Female, age 17

R. Carter, Male, age 17

L. Clarke, Female, age 10

William Clarke, Male, age 17

Mary Collins, Female, age 13

William Coopers, Male, age 16

M. Corbin, Female, age 17

Agnes Crow, Female, age 15

Elizabeth Cullen, Female, age 14

Harriet Curling, Female, age 16

Fanny Davis, Female, age 16

Gilbert Dowley, Male, age 18

William Denby, Male, age 18

B. Dorsey, Male, age 23

B. Ellis, Female, age 16

Rebecca Evans, Female, age 30

Frankey Ferguson, Female, age 40

Ann Fields, Female, age 17

Rheuben Foster, Male age 18

Julia Ann Francis, Female, age 16

Lucy French, Female, age 21

H. Gaines, Male, age 25

Milla Gaines, Female, age 15

H. Garrett, Male age 30

Pompey Garrison, Male, age 19 *

B. Gibson, Male, age 17

Isak Glover, Male age 9

Rachel Glover, Female, age 24

Wiley Glover, Male, age 22

L. Gordon, Female, age 17

George Grandy, Male, age 26 *

Henry Grigsby, Male, age 8

Lucy Grigsby, Female, age 26

E.J. Hardister, Female, age 28

Jacob Haywood, Male, age 17

Mary Hilliard, Female, age 20

Rachel Hanley, Female, age 37

Albert Henning, Male, age 9

Cleo Howard, Female, age 18

James Irvine, Male, age 23

Andrew Jackson, Male, age 24

William Jenkins, Male, age 21 *

Milla Jewett, Female, age 26

Benjamin Johnson, Male, age 23 *

Milinda Joiner, Female, age 21

An infant (name and gender unknown)

Charlotte Jones, Female, age 10

J. Jones, Male, age 22

Phil Jones, Male, age 17 *

Rachel Jones, Female, age 17

Dick (or Nick) King, Male, age 25

Israel King, Male, age 18

Roddy King, Female, age 18

Ruben Knight (or Bright) Male, age 11

Robert Lasey (or Casey) Male, age 19

Margaret Latimore, Female, age 18

Child of Margaret Latimore (age and gender unknown)

Mary Ann Lawson, Female, age 18

Child of Mary Ann Lawson (age and gender unknown)

Arrena Lester, Female, age 15

Harriet Lewis, Female, age 17

John Lindsey, Male, age 21

Mary Lloyd, Female, age 10

Myer Long, Male, age 17

Lewis Lowry, Male, age 21

Robert Lumpkins, Male, age unknown

Leonora Milton, Female, age 9

Bill Moore, Male, age 20

C. Moore, Female, age 19

Elijah Morris, Male, age 23 *

Elizabeth Murdough, Female, age 18

Charles Oliver, Male, age 18

H. Overton, Male, age 33

P. Page, Female, age 17

Ellen (or Eliza) Palmer, Female, age 20

David Parker, Male, age 18

William Parker, Male, age 20

Marshall Pendelton, Male, age 22 *

Jourdon (or Jordon) Phillips, Male, age 21 *

George Portlock, Male, age 21 *

Bob Pullen, Male, age 22

Julia Ray (or Rey), Female, age 13

M. Richardson, Female, age 18

Ginkins Robinson, Male, age 25

Mary Ann Robinson, Female, age 17

Monroe Robinson, Male, age 24

Pinkey Robinson, Female, age 16

Benn Rose, Male, age 17

Dr. Ruffin, Male, age 25 *

Argyle Sales, Male, age 16

Mary E. Scroggins, Female, age 18

William Scott, Male, 10

Violet Scott, Female, age 26

Martha Seatherbury (or Leatherbury), Female, age 13

Lylla Shields, Female, age 11

Susan Shields, Female, age 28

Warner Smith, Male, age 24 *

Alsey Smith, Male, age 24 *

Peter Smallwood, Male, age 23

Edmond Tallafiro, Male, age 21

Martha Thompson, Female, age 22

Addison Tyler, Male, age 23 *

Nelson Walker, Male, age 18

Madison Washington, Male, age 22 *

Sarah Washington, Female, age 15

Henry White, Male, age 23

Monroe White, Male, age 10

P. White, Male, age 18

Winnie Wiley, Male, age 16

Margaret Williams, Female, age 9

William Wilke, Male, age 26

Ann Wilson, Female, age 15

Hester Wilson, Female, age 13

Nelvina Wilson, Female, age 18

H. (or D.) Wood, Male, age 22

America Woodis (or Woodhouse), Male, age 23 *

Mahalia Yancy, Female, age 15

*Indicates the participants in the mutiny.

About The Author

Charles J. (Chuck) Boyle grew up in rural Pennsylvania, entering the army as a private in 1958. He rose swiftly threw the ranks, earning a commission through Infantry Officers Candidate School in 1966. He retired as a Major in 1978. As a second career, Chuck spent more than 20 years as the Senior Army Instructor for Junior Reserve Officer Training, teaching thousands of teenagers good citizenship and leadership at the high school level. He retired from teaching in 2002. He now devotes his time to writing, publishing, and motivational speaking.

Chuck was assigned to Vietnam during 1967-68 where he commanded a platoon in combat. During the Tet Offensive of 1968, he was selected to command Charlie Company, 3rd Battalion, 22nd Infantry, 25th Infantry Division. Among his many awards are two Silver Stars for gallantry in action, two Bronze Stars for heroism, the Purple Heart, and numerous other awards.Chuck received his B.A. in History from the University of Tampa in 1973. Subsequently, he served as Assistant Professor of Military Science at Marion Military Institute in Alabama. He is active in several Vietnam Veterans associations, collecting historical data, writing their histories, and serving as a guest speaker for reunions and social occasions.

Currently he makes his home in Tuscaloosa, Alabama. Chuck is married, has three adult children and nine grandchildren. He has authored "Absolution, Charlie Company, 3rd Battalion, 22nd Infantry," a true story of one man's journey across the battlefields of Vietnam. His recent release of *The Soul of A Slave, Madison Washington and The Creole Mutiny* is a fictionalized account of the life of a slave in the 1840s and his heroic break for freedom.

Chuck has recently co-authored "**The Legend of Mystic Mountain and The Singing Rocks**," an Amazon Kindle eBook for children. He is currently writing "**Is There Anybody Down Range**?" A book about the ten best soldiers he ever met during his 40 years in an Army uniform.

You may enjoy reading this book by Charles J. Boyle

Absolution
Charlie Company, 3rd Battalion, 22nd Infantry
A Vietnam War memoir of ones man's journey across those deadly battlefields.

ISBN 978-0-615-83132-9– Available on Amazon as a hard cover, paperback, and Kindle eBook.

www.ingramcontent.com/pod-product-compliance
Lightning Source LLC
Chambersburg PA
CBHW060231050426
42448CB00009B/1385